Portrait of the
LMS

Published by
Peco Publications and Publicity Ltd.
Seaton, Devon
and printed by
Dawson and Goodall Ltd.,
The Mendip Press, Bath, Somerset

© 1971, V. R. Anderson, R. J. Essery
and D. Jenkinson

Jacket design and frontispiece by
Keith King, depicting an original Royal Scot
in a typical moorland setting

6102

Portrait of the
LMS

by
V. R. Anderson
R. J. Essery
D. Jenkinson

1971 PECO PUBLICATIONS AND PUBLICITY LIMITED

Waiting for the road—LMS style.

Locomotive Class 5XP 'Patriot' 4–6–0 No. 5536 **Private W. Wood, V.C.,** *Circa* 1941

Contents

"Right Away!"—LMS Style

Introduction

The reader might well ask 'Why yet another, mainly pictorial album devoted to the subject of railways?'—and he would be right so to do. We too feel that some sort of apologia is necessary in presenting this 'Portrait of the LMS' so we will explain why it has been compiled.

We have written the work because we feel that between the extremes of a detailed history and the pure 'picture book', there is room for the type of treatment which, while deliberately conceived in an evocative style, still attempts to distil the essence of a railway in a reasonably informative way. All too often, in our experience, the conventional album caption tends to finish at just the point where we would like it to continue a little longer.

We have, therefore, compiled this work as a series of illustrated essays, some very short, others quite long, mostly based on one particular facet of the LMS scene. We have aimed at variety but have made no overt effort to ensure a specific pro-rata quota of space for all parts of the diverse system—indeed this would be impossible. Our subjects are, therefore, personal in the sense that we have felt free to choose the topics from those aspects of the LMS which appeal most to us and we have, on occasion, worn our hearts on our sleeves!

We have made a particular effort to find unpublished pictures and, with a few known exceptions, we feel we have succeeded. For this fact we must offer our sincere thanks to both British Railways and to many other private photographers for allowing us access to and use of items from their collections. Their names are listed at the back of the book. We would also like to thank our many friends for their encouragement and advice—not that we have heeded all of it! Several have contributed pictures and information but we would particularly like to single out T. W. ('Smokey') Bourne for his assistance with information on road vehicles and John Edgington for his kindness in reading the proofs and contributing so many useful facts and suggestions from his encyclopaedic knowledge of all matters LMS. We must also express our gratitude to Keith King for his work on the Jacket design.

Finally, we would like to thank the publisher for doing us the signal honour of asking us to write this, one of the first hard cover works he has undertaken in the publishing field. May his confidence be justified!

What was the LMS?

What was the LMS? The literal answer, so we are told, is that it was, at the time, the largest joint stock corporation operating a railway anywhere in the world. But this answer only begs the question. What *really* was the LMS?

It was a Stanier 'Duchess' on a long train storming unassisted up Beattock or Shap, its rhythmic four-cylinder beat proclaiming to the world that here and nowhere else was the epitome of British steam locomotive design. It was an ex-Midland Class 3F panting up Lickey with that syncopated 'chuff, CHUFF, chuff, chuff' as if it could hardly pull itself, let alone the train—which it left to the unique ten coupled banker 'Big Emma' at the rear, the sound of whose exhaust steam seemed mostly to express sheer relief at having found its way round those incredibly tortuous steam passages! It was one of the grotesquely attractive large boilered Lancashire and Yorkshire 0–8–0s making its way ponderously towards Summit Tunnel from the Yorkshire side with a loaded coal train so long that it beggared the imagination. It was a standard gauge milk tank carried on a narrow gauge transporter wagon on the Leek and Manifold. It was adhesion working on the 1 in 14 of the Cromford and High Peak. It was Compounds and Class 5s thrashing their way up to Blea Moor or Peak Forest. It was an elderly ex-LNWR 4–4–0 reviving memories of departed glory as it sprinted along the North Wales coast with a Llandudno local. It was a Lanky 0–6–0 operating in mid-Wales. It was a Highland 'Ben' piloting a Stanier Class 5 over Britain's highest main line summit. It was the 'Sou-West' having to share a bed with the 'Caley'!

What was the LMS? It was all these things and many more. Basically, however, it was a veneer of standardised parts and practices added, after 1922, to a variety of different patterns already so well incised during most of the previous 100 years that they could never be totally eliminated. It was, if you like, a shotgun marriage of often incompatible partners and was sometimes called, quite wrongly, 'Greater Derby'. But, withal, it was a great railway. By the supreme irony of appointing a Swindon man, it took up locomotive design where the GWR had called 'finis' and so improved the breed that Swindon eventually *had* to take note! It made what were conceivably the best general service passenger coaches in the country (and, let it not be denied, a few of the worst!) and fed their occupants with probably the best meals on rails to be found in these islands.

Its constituents had styled themselves with fine conceit by such titles as 'Premier Line', 'The Best Way' and so on. To all these the LMS fell heir and, it is fair to add, probably justified most of them.

What was the LMS? The question cannot be answered simply but in the following pages we have tried to select some of the answers out of the many hundreds which could legitimately be given.

Symbolising the LMS at its zenith, Stanier Coronation Class 4–6–2 No. 6254 **City of Stoke-on-Trent**, leaving **Carlisle** with a Euston express at the very start of the BR period, makes a quite remarkable contrast with the scene at **St. Pancras** less than 20 years earlier when engines such as ex-MR Kirtley 0–4–4T No. 1219 were still very much in evidence. When Stanier was born, the Kirtley was over six years old; yet by the time it reached the scrapheap in 1935, Stanier was 59 and had designed all but one of his standard range of locomotives! This, in a nutshell, is what the LMS was all about . . .

Hors d'oeuvres

1. Contrasts

It is hard to believe that the upper picture was taken as late as 11th June 1932. It shows LMS standard Class 3F 0–6–0T No. 16570 (later 7487) on a 13 coach set of possibly the most archaic coaches inherited by the company. They were ex-North London Railway four-wheelers and the train is seen passing **Cemetery box** on that section of the LNER (ex-GNR) line over which the NLR had operated its trains.

Only three years later saw the Silver Jubilee of King George V but the LMS failed to mark it in quite the same spectacular way as did the LNER with its streamlined trains. However, the event did not pass entirely unnoticed and the fruit of the LMS effort is seen passing **Kilburn** (below) on 10th May 1935 in the shape of Stanier Class 5XP No. 5552 **Silver Jubilee**. This engine started life as 5642 and ran as such in red livery for four months before being selected as the prototype for naming, thus becoming the recipient of not only the special black and chrome livery but also the pioneer running number for the class as a whole. The external state of the engine plus the fact that it is on a stopping train suggests that it had only just entered revenue service.

During the early years of the LMS, much more general merchandise was conveyed in sheeted down open wagons than was ever conveyed in covered vans. This is well exemplified by the picture (above) of a typical LMS express freight on ex-Lancashire and Yorkshire territory, circa 1930. The locomotive, No. 12596, is a Hughes superheated belpaire rebuild of an earlier Aspinall design. Its LYR number was 1599. Note the open carriage truck marshalled as the third vehicle of the train.

By virtue of the fact that both the Midland and the LNWR had managed to gain access to the city, the LMS was in a position to mount a 'pincer movement' for traffic from the Great Western stronghold at Swansea. The picture below shows Stanier Class 5 No. 5191 leaving the ex-LNWR terminus at **Swansea Victoria** with a northbound express probably bound for Shrewsbury. For the first mile or two of its journey it travelled alongside the lines of the Swansea and Mumbles railway. To the right of this picture ran the ex-LNWR goods branch to Swansea Docks station.

2. Premier Line

Ex-LNWR employees may have felt that their old company had come off worst in its battle for supremacy with the Midland in early LMS days, but the fact remained that the old North Western route from Euston was always pre-eminent as a generator of express passenger traffic. As a result, the newest coaches generally went first to the Euston services and the line itself became the almost exclusive preserve of the larger and more glamorous express passenger locomotives like the original Royal Scots and Pacifics. Above is shown the classic view of **Tring cutting** with parallel boiler Royal Scot 4–6–0 No. 6159 **The Royal Air Force**, working hard with a southbound express circa 1937.

The slow lines swung away from the fast roads at **Watford tunnels** and the picture below, taken on 5th August 1935, shows the two sets of lines converging again just north of the tunnel portals. The train is a down local headed by Stanier three-cylinder Class 4P 2–6–4T No. 2504. These engines were later to be confined almost exclusively to the Tilbury line (see page 53) but until bridge strengthening had been completed, they were used on several parts of the system.

3. The Best Way

The Midland's riposte to the LNWR 'Premier Line' claim was a somewhat more subtle but less harmonious phrase. However, in spite of having its own way about livery and other ephemera, the Midland was very much Number Two when it came to the allocation of new and more powerful motive power after the grouping. Nevertheless, during the 1930s, two of the new LMS standard classes became very much associated with the Midland main line. Both are depicted here.

Although not confined to the St. Pancras route, the Stanier Jubilees did, nevertheless, make this line very much their own preserve. The striking view of No. 5709 **Implacable** (above) heading the northbound 'Thames-Forth Express' circa 1937–8 was taken at the approaches to **Luton.**

The LMS Garratts were even more at home on the Midland Division, never working regularly anywhere else. Below is shown No. 4992 heading north past **Elstree** with a Brent to Toton train of coal empties on 5th May 1937.

4. North of the Border

If the LNWR was the Premier Line, the Caley was very much the 'Royal Route'—it even purloined the Royal Coat of Arms for use on its engines! It had some particularly robust locomotives which seemed to last for ever and this may have been one of the reasons why LMS standard types did not seem to come onto its lines quite so often in early days. Some of the exceptions to this longevity were the massive but beautifully proportioned McIntosh 4–6–0s. Two of them are seen in this picture leaving **Aberdeen** in the early LMS period. The engines are 'Cardean' Class 4–6–0s No. 14754 (ex-CR 905), leading and No. 14753 (ex-CR 904) next to the train.

'**Gleneagles** for Auchterarder West and Junction for Crieff, Comrie and St. Fillans' ran the legend on the platform in the palmy days when ex-CR lines seemed to occupy most valleys of consequence between Perth and Crainlarich. Entering the branch loop during the 1930s is McIntosh 'Dunalastair IV' Class 4–4–0 No. 14459 (ex-CR 42) with a down express. Today, only the main line to Perth remains open while the golfers bound for the nearby LMS built Gleneagles Hotel almost certainly go by car!

During later LMS days, Scotland eventually received its quota of LMS standard engines. In the adjoining picture, Stanier Class 3P 2–6–2T No. 185 is seen at **Grantown-on-Spey** in 1939, complete with snowplough and a one coach local (an ex-LNWR corridor brake composite). The ex-HR line from Aviemore to Forres via Grantown and Dava was, until the cut-off line via Slocht Summit was built, the main route from Perth to Inverness and for many many years after the shorter route was built, long distance trains from the south divided at Aviemore in order to serve both routes. The reverse procedure was followed in the southbound direction but now, alas, Grantown is yet another Scottish resort which will never hear again the sounds of a railway train.

5. Behind the Scenes

An interior view of the signal box at **Dore and Totley Station Junction**—the meeting point of the Sheffield–Manchester and Sheffield–Derby main lines of the Midland Railway. The box and its equipment are of pure Midland design.

Camping coaches are nothing new—but the LMS called them 'Caravans'. In this picture, three ex-MR and one ex-LYR coaches are receiving the finishing touches and being equipped for the coming season at **Derby works**. There is little visible external evidence of the change in role of the coaches.

In the days before instant pre-packed, quick frozen everything, the preparation of food for the dining car services was a formidable task. This view shows the food preparation room at the **Euston Dining Car Depot** at about the time of the grouping. The list of services to be provisioned was chalked up on the board to the left of the door. Honesty compels one to wonder if the Public Health Inspector ever ventured through the doors !

6. Claughton Metamorphosis

The original four-cylinder LNWR Claughton Class 4–6–0 (see page 101), was not an entirely satisfactory machine and amongst its defects was a rather too small boiler. The LMS made two attempts to improve matters. The first, in 1928, was to rebuild 20 of them with larger boilers. Ten retained their Walschaerts valve gear but the other ten were fitted with Beardmore-Caprotti valve gear to enable comparative tests to be made. A truly imposing engine resulted from the conversion and Caprotti rebuild No. 5948 **Baltic** (above) made a fine picture as she stood at **Willesden** on 17th September 1932.

The reboilering was not an unqualified success and a much more drastic rebuild involving the same larger boiler but a totally new three-cylinder chassis (based on that of the Royal Scot Class) was initiated in 1930. The outcome was the 'Baby Scot' 4–6–0, somewhat more officially referred to as the 'Patriot' Class in later years. With the possible exception of the first two locomotives, the Patriots were more in the nature of 'accountancy rebuilds', there being very little, if any, Claughton left in the finished product. However, the first 42 to be 'built' took the running numbers of the Claughtons they had, nominally, replaced. No. 5933 (later 5521 **Rhyl**) is seen below at **Kentish Town** on 2nd September 1933. In 1934, all the 42 locomotives, together with ten more new ones, were numbered into the 5500–51 series. The Stanier Jubilee Class was, in effect, the taper boiler equivalent of the Patriot.

7. Inspired by Stanier

Stanier left the LMS in fact, if not in name, during the early war years but his influence lived on. The Converted Royal Scots (above) and the Fairburn 2–6–4Ts (below), designed in 1943 and 1945 respectively, both bore the unmistakeable hallmarks of the genius from Swindon who had so revolutionised LMS motive power during the 1930s. No. 6150 **The Life Guardsman** was photographed at **Manchester London Road** in 1946 and No. 2239, complete with Caledonian type route indicator on the centre lamp iron at **Glasgow Central** in 1947.

Stations large and small

To most people, a station is simply a place where one waits to board a train. That it may or may not have character or even possess points of interest is small consolation if the train is late, the station is draughty or it is raining! Even so, the fact that it is the principal point of contact between the railway and most of its customers makes it a little surprising that the station has been relatively neglected in railway literature. A humble attempt to slightly rectify this state of affairs is made in the next few pages.

Heath Park Halt—ex-MR Hemel Hempstead branch. This diminutive facility is thought to be possibly the smallest LMS station regularly used by passengers. Blackwell Mill was actually the smallest but had only one weekly train and was not in the public timetable. The LMS standard 'Hawkseye' nameboard is worthy of note for so small a stopping place.

The LMS inherited most of its stations but it did build a few, of which **Apsley** on the main line out of Euston was one example. The station was built to cater for the large business generated by Dickinson & Company's mills and the growing residential development in the area between King's Langley and Boxmoor.

The station was formally opened on 22nd September 1938 by a train running through a large paper hoop suspended from the station roof! Appropriately enough, the paper was made by John Dickinson & Co. whose chairman, Sir Reginald Bonsor, Bt., received the first ticket, serial 000 and punched by Lord Stamp no less. Opened to the public four days later, the station made extensive use of reinforced and pre-cast concrete. The original description of the station refers to the attractive colour schemes adopted including the mulberry coloured surface brick, cream coloured mortar and bright emerald window frames!

It is rare that one can find pictures of a station at three stages of its career but these three views, fortuitously, show **Morecambe Promenade** before, during and after LMS ownership.

Though not quite complete, it was first opened on Sunday 24th March 1907 to cater for the Easter traffic. The old station, being too small and inconvenient, had militated against the prosperity of the town by virtue of the delays experienced in handling traffic. In 1944, Modern Transport described the station as a '. . . combination in the late Victorian style of neo-Tudor Gothic with a roof of iron and glass embellished by creeper and hanging flower baskets.'

The new station was designed to handle a volume of traffic far in excess of anything that had yet been carried to the shores of Morecambe Bay. The buildings were imposing and in keeping with the sea front amenities of the day and the whole structure was designed along similar lines to Bradford Forster Square. The glass-roofed circulating area was 174ft × 50ft.

The upper picture shows the station in MR days very soon after opening in 1907. Note that the creepers are already in position against the buttresses. The centre view, of LMS vintage, shows much more foliage, a more imposing bookstall and the inevitable rash of enamel advertisements below the cornice mouldings. Note that the LMS saw fit to retain the MR station signs but replaced the MR hanging gas lamps with replacements to its own, not entirely unpleasing design—still gas however.

BR, on the other hand, gave the station a more spacious appearance by removing the signs and pruning the creepers (lower view). However, the replacement electric lamp shades can only be regarded as an unqualified aesthetic disaster!

Unfortunately, 'in period' pictures of LMS railway stations are relatively rare. These four small country stations were all photographed in recent years.

The main station building at **Cockermouth** on the Cockermouth, Keswick and Penrith Railway was quite an imposing affair. It was matched by the equally ornate wooden platform shelter on the westbound platform depicted in this view.

Not even its friends could claim that the Lancashire and Yorkshire Railway had the most attractive stations in the Kingdom. However, some of the more rural establishments (or should one say 'less urban'?), had a modicum of charm. Such a station was **Blackrod** at the junction of the Horwich branch.

The Furness and Midland railways had little in common, except an odd stretch of joint line, but when they opted for cottage style station architecture, the results were often surprisingly similar. The upper picture depicts **Silverdale** station, the first stop out of Carnforth on the Furness line to Barrow and the lower picture is of **Whatstandwell** on the Derby–Manchester main line of the Midland Railway just north of Ambergate.

Kingscliffe station on the ex-LNWR Market Harborough to Peterborough line, shown here in later LMS days, was a somewhat more harmonious design than many ex-LNWR stations. Oddly enough, the buildings and track layout seem to be more reminiscent of the Midland than the North Western. Note that although taken some 15 years after grouping, most of the station 'furniture' (nameboards, signs, signalbox &c.) is still pure LNWR.

Byfield was a typical station on that almost forgotten stretch of the LMS, the Stratford-upon-Avon and Midland Junction Railway. It was opened in 1873. The signal box was constructed by the Railway Signal Company but the nameboards are of LMS design. Indicative of the minor nature of the route in LMS days is the state of the track. It seems to be mostly made up from somewhat worn 45ft rail sections.

Wemyss Bay, on the shores of the Firth of Clyde, was one of the embarkation points for holidaymaking Glaswegian and tourist alike. It was furnished with a graceful Caledonian covered station which made extensive use of glass and iron tracery. The photograph was taken in LMS days and also shows the covered approach to the boarding point for the Clyde Coast Steamers.

Portpatrick station just a few miles past Stranraer, was the rudimentary terminus at the head of the Portpatrick and Wigtownshire Joint Railway. This line, which ran to Castle Douglas with a branch to Garlieston and Whithorn, was jointly owned by the CR, GSWR, LNWR and MR—one of the only two instances of a purely Scottish line being under the part ownership of English companies, the other being, of course, the Forth Bridge Railway. The Stranraer—Portpatrick stretch was, in reality, only a minor branch of the system since the most important trains, including all the boat trains for the short sea crossing to Ireland, terminated at Stranraer. All local services were operated jointly by the CR and GSWR and the picture shows ex-CR 0–6–0 'Jumbo' No. 17440 (ex-CR 571), fitted with tender cab, at the head of a local train of pre-group stock.

Culloden Moor was the first stop out of Inverness on the direct Highland Railway route to Aviemore via Slochtd. This picture, looking south, though taken in late LMS days, still has much ex-HR atmosphere about it in the shape of the signal box, station nameboard, lamps and, of course, the magnificent setting. The break in the down gradient prior to reaching the viaduct is very noticeable. Halfway over the viaduct the line swings right and makes for Daviot. Looking back from the train at this point gave the passenger one of the finest scenic views on the whole LMS system.

The LNWR pushed several tentacles down the valleys of North Wales from its Chester and Holyhead main line. Most of them passed through delectable scenery and the line from Llandudno to Blaenau Ffestiniog was no exception. In the picture below, a Webb 0–6–0 is seen entering the delightfully rural station at **Tal-y-Cafn** with the Welsh mountains as a backdrop.

TAL-Y-CAFN
EGLWYSBACH

Ripley Station (above) was at the head of the seven mile single track section of the old Midland Railway from Little Eaton Junction just north of Derby. It was one of the localities selected by the LMS for the experimental evaluation of Sentinel steam railcars c. 1925–6. This particular railcar is thought to have gone to the Jersey Eastern Railway but the LMS later purchased examples for its own use. Amongst the station details can be noted the ex-MR signs, gaslamps, platform seats and signal-box nameboard. The signal box itself is of 'middle period' Midland design.

Cricklewood station (below) was a typical stopping place on the London extension of the Midland Railway. Amongst the signs of LMS ownership on this picture are the upper quadrant signals on the right and the Fowler 2–6–2 tank on the left. Note particularly the milk tanks in the Express Dairy sidings. These were worked in daily from parts of the country as far afield as Appleby.

Bow Station (above) was constructed in characteristically lavish North London style. This picture was taken in 1929 when, according to the billboards, one could get to Arsenal for 5d or to Derbyshire for 7/6d return!

The building contained, apart from the usual booking hall and station offices, a library, reading room, classrooms and a concert hall seating 800. Known as the Bow and Bromley Institute it was the largest and best equipped hall in the East End. Its popularity declined after the opening of the Queen's Hall and it finally became part Billiard hall and part mission. In front stands the Bryant and May Memorial Fountain, erected by public subscription to commemorate the successful exertions by Bryant and May (whose factory is close by) to defeat a proposal to put a tax on matches!

Below, **Southport Chapel Street** shows the marks of three owners. It has the LYR motif in the tracery, LMS at the ends of the canopy and BR headed notice boards. This was an immensely busy station. From June to September 1935, almost $1\frac{1}{2}$ million tickets were collected and on summer Saturdays, 475 regular trains were booked in and out—not to mention excursions. In addition, Southport was a seaside dormitory town for Lancashire businessmen and had residential services to many of the large industrial towns.

'Holbeck Loco.' (20A). Holbeck, Leeds, was the principal depot in an area which covered the ex-MR main line from Royston in the south to Lancaster in the north-west. Holbeck was a typical Midland 'round' shed with the engine house arranged in the form of a series of turntables, each with numerous shed roads radiating from it like the spokes of a wheel. In the background of this picture can be seen the entrances to the turntables within the engine house. In the foreground is an interesting assortment of ex-MR and LMS standard locomotive types—one suspects that the railwaymen were posed specially! The picture was taken on 13th July 1939 and noteworthy is the variety of liveries to be seen displayed on the locomotives (Red: 5621; Lined Black: 1428, 177, 5302; Plain Black: 322(3?), 3944). Note also the short lived 1936–7 sans serif insignia on 1428 and 5302.

On shed

Big sheds, little sheds, old sheds, new sheds, the LMS had them all. But what, precisely, constituted an LMS locomotive shed? One thing was certain, it was not simply the building inside which the locomotives were housed. As far as the LMS was concerned, the phrase 'Engine Shed' was rarely used. The officially favoured term was Motive Power Depot and the covered building in which some of the engines reposed was, more correctly, termed the 'engine house'. LMS mpds existed to 'garage, repair and maintain' its stock of locomotives. For about ten years after grouping, the old pre-group pattern was maintained but in the mid-1930s, the LMS introduced a rationalised motive power system based on a limited number of principal depots and dozens of sub-sheds, usually called 'garage' depots.

Each principal area was in the charge of a District Locomotive Superintendent and was allocated a reference number. All mpds in that area carried the same number, being distinguished from each other by different suffix letters. Thus, Macclesfield (9C) was a garage depot in Area Number 9 whose main depot was Manchester Longsight (9A). The locomotives carried their depot of allocation on a cast metal smokebox plate. Not only were the sheds rationalised in this way, but the LMS also instituted a considerable programme of modernisation at many of its larger depots in order to reduce repair and maintenance costs and generally tighten up the whole accounting procedures relating to the locomotive stock. In the next few pages an attempt is made to show something of the LMS shed scene during the years.

Polmadie (27A), above, was the principal ex-Caledonian Railway depot on the outskirts of Glasgow. Its garage depots at the time of this picture (November 1947), were at Greenock and Hamilton. The picture in addition to showing a mixture of LMS standard and ex-Caledonian engines, is also interesting as showing the coaling plant and, in the foreground, the elevator belt from the many ashpits in the middle distance.

Royston (20C), below, is of chief interest in illustrating the fact that a garage shed was not necessarily a small depot. In fact, Royston was important enough for the LMS to open a new depot there in 1931 and this picture was taken to show the new engine house and other facilities installed there.

26

Another large sub-shed was the old LNWR depot at **Stafford** (5C), above. This depot had a parallel road engine house which was more economical of space than the Midland roundhouse type. Although it was not quite so easy to get any particular locomotive out of this type of shed, the type was much favoured by the LNWR. The principal point of interest here is the new concrete built mechanical coaling plant on the right. As part of its rationalisation process, the LMS installed these plants at many of its larger depots.

Holyhead (7C) was quite a small garage shed of the main depot at Llandudno Junction. However, as the picture below shows, it was host to some of the impressive motive power used by the LMS on its Irish boat traffic. Seen here are Royal Scots 6161 **Kings Own** and 6155 **The Lancer** together with Stanier Class 5 No. 5111 and an unidentified ex-LNWR George the Fifth Class 4–4–0. On the left, another unidentified 'George' heads a local train (composed of an 'inter-district set' of LMS standard non-corridor lavatory stock) towards Holyhead station.

The LMS had its share of small locomotive depots and four widely scattered examples are shown on this page.

Above (left) is **Tewkesbury**, a substantially built 'one engine' house on the ex-MR branch from Ashchurch to Malvern. The view is taken facing west and shows the unusual arrangement whereby the line to the old passenger station passed between the two tall buildings. The picture was taken in September 1949 and the engine is ex-MR Class 3F 0–6–0 No. 43506.

Above right is the ex-MR facility at **Ingleton** which closed in April 1954. Most Midland sheds, even the small ones, were quite substantial structures (e.g. Wirksworth— page 58), so this wooden building was a little unusual. Note the characteristic MR pattern water tank with a not so characteristic water hose sticking out below it from the wooden supporting structure. The buffer stop in the foreground is distinctly elaborate even by MR standards.

To the left are depicted two small Scottish sheds. The upper view shows **Crieff** (ex-CR) at the junction of the branches from Perth and Gleneagles. The presence of two engine houses at one small depot was not typical, even if each of them could only hold one locomotive! The picture was taken on 21st June 1935.

One of the most familiar of the ex-HR depots was the shed at **Kyle of Lochalsh**. This was a two road stone built structure and the most westerly LMS locomotive depot on the mainland of Great Britain. The picture is undated but was almost certainly taken in pre-Stanier days— or, at least, before the Black 5s had begun to monopolise the traffic on the Kyle line. The locomotives in the picture are Cumming designed ex-HR 4–6–0 'Clan Goods' Nos. 17951 (ex-HR 76) and 17953 (ex-HR 78).

These two pictures of **Cricklewood** typify the transformation wrought by the LMS at many of its larger mpds during the 1930s. Above is shown the original manual coaling stage in early post-group days, still redolent with Midland Railway atmosphere in the shape of the gaslamps and water cranes. Note also the vast variety of the wagon stock, the pre-group livery on some of the vehicles and the sand wagons in the foreground.

The picture below was taken from the same place in 1931. The old coaling stage is a heap of rubble and has been replaced by a new mechanical plant seen in the background. The rows of wagons are still present but the variety has considerably decreased.

The coaling stage at **Plaistow** (ex-LT & SR)—opposite—was a unique and striking structure. However, the semi-mechanised coaling system was not untypical of practice at several depots at the time of grouping. The coal was unloaded from the wagons by hand but fed into the locomotive bunker by means of the mechanical conveyor belt. Judging by the size of the lump of coal about to descend into the bunker of No. 2102, the fireman was destined for some hard work!

Both locomotives are genuine Tilbury types. No. 2227 was an 0–6–2T (ex-LT&SR 76, ex-MR 2187). It became 2187 again in 1939 and 1987 in 1947. No. 2102 was a Whitelegg 4–6–4T designed for the LT&SR but not delivered until after the MR took over in 1912. It was later renumbered 2194 before scrapping in 1929.

On this page are shown rather more up to date methods of coal handling. The wagon tippler (above) saved enormous amounts of hard work at the sheds and the coal was carried by conveyor belt to the top of the coaling plant and hence by gravity to the engines. The photograph was taken at **Wellingborough** (ex-MR).

To the right is shown the even more elaborate mechanical coaler at **Farnley Junction** (ex-LNWR), disgorging a rather dusty looking load into the tender of Stanier Class 5 No. 5085. It will be readily appreciated how much of a saving in time and money was achieved by the company with these improvements when compared with the older methods shown opposite.

The observant visitor to a shed could always find more to attract his interest than the mere presence of any particular locomotive—fortunately, some visitors recorded their observations photographically.

Above left is shown in close-up, the rear of ex-LYR 0–6–0ST No. 11342 (ex-LYR 249). The particular point of interest is the presence of the fireirons festooned round the lamp brackets. It was always a problem to know where to put these implements on a saddle tank. Tender engines carried them on the tender itself (see below) and side tank engines usually had the fireirons on top of the flat side tanks themselves.

Above right is a close-up view of an LMS standard compound in the 109x series. The main feature to be noted is the bare patch of paint above the short grab handle on the tender. This was caused by steam still blowing out of the slaking pipe after footplate washing down operations.

Finally (below) is a picture specially taken to show how *not* to coal up a tender engine! One can imagine the fireman having an unenviable task trying to shovel the coal from the front of this particular tender. The locomotive is ex-MR compound No. 1033 fitted with replacement Stanier chimney but paired with an ex-MR Deeley standard tender (the fore-runner of the Fowler type).

One of the dirtiest jobs to be found 'on shed' was the disposal of a locomotive after it had worked its appointed roster. In particular, the cleaning out and removal of smokebox and firebox ash was a tiresome chore. As with coaling, the LMS also streamlined its ash disposal methods. The ash conveyor at Polmadie has already been mentioned (page 26) and above are two more examples. On the left, a Fowler LMS standard Class 7F 0–8–0 is having the smokebox soot and ash shovelled out by hand prior to removal in one of the little hopper wagons on the right of the picture. The location is **Hillhouse** depot, Hudders-field (ex-LNWR/LYR joint) circa 1939.

Above right is shown the mechanised ash plant at **Toton** (ex-MR). The ash was tipped directly from the trolleys into the disposal wagons by means of a simple elevator.

Oil firing was far less messy than coal but the LMS only adopted it for a short time in the 1920s at about the time of the General Strike. Below left is shown LMS standard compound No. 1136 being refuelled. Note that the refuelling is being effected direct from a tank wagon.

Boiler 'wash-out' day was a feature of most LMS depots of any significance. Hughes 4–6–4T No. 11117 is seen here at **Agecroft** in April 1939 with the wash out hose still in position. These engines were LMS built derivatives of the Hughes LYR design 4–6–0 tender engines.

'Garaging, repair and maintenance' was the main function of the LMS mpd and the pictures on this page concentrate on the 'repair and maintenance' aspect. Below, a Stanier Class 8F is seen undergoing attention to its motion while 'on shed'. Note particularly the 'scotches' inserted below the wheel treads to prevent the wheels moving and also the 'target' board projecting from the tender which indicated to the shed staff that the engine was not to be moved. Part of the motion lies on the ground alongside the engine.

Two other repair situations are depicted in the above pictures. At the top, ex-LYR steam railmotor No. 10601 (ex-LYR 4) is seen without its wheels. These units, of 0–4–0 wheel arrangement, formed the front end only of the railmotor. When the engine part was in need of repair it was possible to attach the passenger carrying portion to another serviceable engine unit.

The final picture shows LMS standard compound No. 1134 over the wheel drop at **Perth** in August 1939. Quite substantial repairs could be effected at many sheds and this frequently prevented the necessity of sending the locomotive into the main works for overhaul.

34

The LYR had amalgamated with the LNWR one year before the grouping and at the northern end of the old LNWR main line, the Hughes LYR designed 4–6–0s (better known as Lanky 'Dreadnoughts' or sometimes even as Lanky 'Claughtons') quickly took over some of the workings formerly performed by ex-LNWR classes. The upper picture shows No. 10451 in newly acquired red livery descending past the familiar towering LNWR signals at **Oxenholme** circa 1924–5 with an up West Coast express. This particular engine, like the one in the second picture, did not enter service until 1923 and for the first few months of its career ran in non-standard livery with its pre-group series number 1680. It is noteworthy that only the first two coaches are passenger carrying vehicles, the second being an ex-WCJS 12-wheeler.

The second picture also taken in the mid-1920s, shows another Hughes 4–6–0 (No. 10438, built in 1923 as No. 1667) on what might almost be called its home metals as it heads inland past **Lea Road troughs** on the Preston and Wyre main line. The train is a returning excursion from Blackpool composed mainly of ex-LYR high roof non-corridor stock. On the nearer track, another returning excursion train, composed mainly of 48ft ex-Midland low roof gaslit non-corridor stock, is headed by ex-MR Class 4 0–6–0 No. 4024.

On the lesser LNWR lines, nothing much changed, save for the livery, for several years after grouping. The lower picture taken circa 1928, shows ex-LNWR 2–4–0 No. 5020 **Delhi** (ex-LNWR 1674) in plain black livery leaving **Whitchurch**, Salop, with a local train composed of ex-LNWR arc roof non-corridor stock dating from the 1890s.

Although LNWR coaches fairly quickly assumed LMS livery, many of the ex-LNWR locomotives did not, partly due to a considerable re-organisation of Crewe Works at the time.

When re-numbering was resumed, considerations of speed decreed that many ex-LNWR passenger engines were returned to service without a red repaint and by the time *this* picture was taken, the company had officially decided to adopt black for all its locomotives except the main express passenger types. The locomotive number was placed on the cabside and not the tender after this change in livery policy.

In Scotland, there was less reluctance to use the new LMS colours than had been the case in the ex-LNWR areas and although, initially, the trains themselves showed little change, the new colours were quickly applied throughout what became known as the Northern Division of the LMS.

Of all the locomotives and rolling stock which came to the LMS from its Scottish constituents, those that belonged to the Glasgow and South Western were probably the least resilient. Such scenes as are depicted in the first two pictures on this page were to be seen for only a short period after the grouping. The upper picture, taken at **Glasgow St. Enoch**, presents a strange contrast of old and new. The locomotive, Whitelegg 4–6–4T No. 15402 (ex-GSWR 542) was built only one year before the grouping but the train was composed of somewhat outdated gaslit six-wheelers, the oldest of which probably rivalled those of the old North London Railway (see page 10) in terms of antiquated looks.

A similar train is seen in the second picture, taken at **Ibrox** on the G&P Joint Line. The locomotive in this case probably matched some of the coaches for age. Introduced in 1893, these neat Manson designed 0–4–4Ts were to have a relatively short life in LMS days, all being scrapped by 1932. The engine depicted, No. 15252, was ex-GSWR No. 527.

Up on the Highland main line, the cavalcades of assorted stock from all parts of the Kingdom continued to be worked north of Perth by Jones, Drummond and Cumming designed engines for several years. Lochgorm works at Inverness, seemed to take particular pride in the application of the new red livery to the ex-HR locomotives which, taken all in all, seemed to wear the style very well. A good example of this is provided by the leading engine of a southbound stopping train seen entering **Luncarty** on the ex-Caledonian owned connecting link between the end of the Highland line at Stanley Junction and the joint station at Perth. The locomotive is Jones Loch Class 4–4–0 No. 14384 **Loch Laggan** (ex-HR 124) and the train engine is an unidentified Drummond Castle Class 4–6–0. Characteristically, the leading coach appears to be of NBR origin!

The ex-Midland part of the LMS changed more slowly. In part, of course, this was because of the large scale adoption of Midland practices by the LMS (Locomotive designs, coach designs, livery etc). However, another contributory factor to the apparently changeless nature of the Midland scene was the extraordinary longevity of many of the locomotives.

Virtually the only indication of LMS ownership in the adjoining picture is the presence of two LMS standard lavatory brake thirds in the formation of a down local circa 1930. The locomotive still in red livery, is one of Johnson's classic 1400 Class 2–4–0s, No. 240, with Deeley smokebox and chimney. The leading coach is a low roofed gaslit Clayton 12 wheel lavatory third with luggage compartment.

In 1928, the red livery was officially abandoned for most locomotive classes and the ex-MR 4–4–0s depicted in the two adjacent pictures were both sporting the then fairly new lined black livery when seen on trains at **York**. However, apart from the locomotive livery, there is little evidence of post-group period save, perhaps, for the ex-LNWR coaches behind the tender of No. 370.

Another aspect of Midland policy which did not change over much after the LMS was formed was the continuous and be-wildering rebuilding of ex-MR locomotives. Both 4–4–0s in this picture dated from the 1880s, at which time they exhibited the far more graceful lines of the original Johnson design. No. 368 is the Deeley saturated rebuild of 1904 vintage with Belpaire boiler and extended smokebox while No. 370, having already gone through an identical pro-cess, has been further rebuilt to the final superheated Fowler condition. Both locomotives were shedded at Hasland at the time of the pictures (circa 1928–30) which makes it highly probable that the trains were serving either the Chesterfield or Derby area via the Swinton and Knottingley joint line.

By contrast with conventional trains, the LMS also operated a number of electrified services in London and the North-West. Above is shown a six-coach train of the well-known ex-LNWR London area Oerlikon stock as running in early LMS days . . . not, perhaps, looking quite as elegant as in its pre-group colours but still very smart in the fully lined LMS style. Although the LMS built some new compartment stock to supplement these pre-group sets, they never really surpassed the Oerlikons in public esteem.

At about the same point in time, the lower picture was taken. It shows ex-LNWR observation car No. 5316 on crew training duty between **Llandudno Junction** and **Blaenau Ffestiniog** in the happy days before motor cars and road coaches had killed all such attempts to stimulate tourist traffic. The car was built in 1913 at Wolverton as LNWR 1503 and it became LMS 15843 in 1933. Withdrawn in November 1962, it has, fortunately, been preserved on the Bluebell line. The rest of the train is made up of a typically motley collection of ex-LNWR six-wheelers.

The LMS was economy minded and it was not long before the lesser branches were given a critical examination by the Lord Stamp regime. However, for quite a number of years, the company did make some attempt to operate what were fast becoming liabilities rather than assets. Typical of the LMS branch line scene was the nicely venerable pair of ex-MR coaches doing duty on the **Hemel Hempstead** branch in 1929 (above). The locomotive is ex-MR Johnson Class 1F 0–6–0T No. 1669.

The Somerset and Dorset was not, of course, regarded as an 'unremunerative branch line' until long after its demise as an independent concern in 1930. In that year, it was 'divided' between the LMS and Southern railways. The LMS acquired all the locomotives but the two companies shared the coaching stock. Although some of the locomotives lasted for a very long time, the LMS did not seem very enthusiastic about its newly acquired passenger vehicles (perhaps their outline was a bit too South Western for all tastes!) At all events they were quickly scrapped.

The lower picture, taken at **Highbridge** in July 1930, shows Johnson 0–4–4T No. 1207 (ex-S&D 31A) at the head of a two coach motor-fitted train of ex-S&D coaches. The whole ensemble is still in S&D blue livery. Although the engine has had its old ownership markings erased, the coaches still carry full S&D insignia in the waist panelling. It was only the small letters LMS in the lower right corners of the side panelling which, presumably, distinguished them from the coaches which went to the Southern.

By the early 1930s, a sort of pattern was emerging. The more important services were now being handled by standard locomotives and stock while the pre-group equipment was to some extent beginning to be confined to lesser duties. Typical of what was to be seen is the above picture of the down 'Royal Scot' at **Watford** in 1931.

The massive 16 coach train is composed almost entirely of the recently introduced and very handsome 'middle period' coaching stock. These coaches, which many hold to be the most stylish of all the LMS designs, introduced large 'picture' windows to the LMS and they had no outside compartment doors. The locomotives are LMS standard Class 4P compound 4–4–0 No. 1118 and Royal Scot Class 6P 4–6–0 No. 6137, at that time named **Vesta**.

Typifying many of the local trains of similar vintage is ex-MR Johnson Belpaire Class 3P 4–4–0 No. 767 at **Elstree** in August 1933 with a Bedford–St. Pancras local. The train consists of three ex-MR 48ft low roof suburban coaches of David Bain design but with a high elliptical roof brake third bringing up the rear.

42

The photo at the top shows Princess Royal Class 4-6-2, No. 6206 *Princess Marie Louise* at Bushey.

By the later 1930s, LMS standard loco-motives were working nearly all the principal expresses and flush sided Stanier pattern coaches were becoming widespread. Compare, for example, the coaches in the above picture of the down 'Royal Scot' at **Bushey** in the later 1930s with the vehicles in the same train only a few years earlier as shown on the previous page. The locomotive is now one of the main batch of Stanier Princess Royal Class 4–6–2s, No. 6206 **Princess Marie Louise**.

Earlier LMS standard engines were now rostered to other workings and the lower picture shows a typical Patriot turn. The train is a down express of Southern Railway stock from the south coast, again at **Bushey** troughs, and the locomotive is No. 5509.

The LMS contribution to the streamline era of the 1930s was the 'Coronation Scot' introduced in 1937. Above is shown the southbound train in the Lancashire area behind Stanier streamlined pacific No. 6223 **Princess Alice**. This train was finished in bright blue livery with horizontal silver stripes.

In late 1938, the LMS resolved to replace the 1937 sets with new trains of specially built articulated stock. These were planned to enter service in 1940 but the decision to build them stemmed from a wish to demonstrate the 'Coronation Scot' at the New York World Fair of 1939. The locomotive selected was No. 6229 **Duchess of Hamilton**, one of the second batch of streamliners but, for publicity reasons, it exchanged identity with No. 6220 **Coronation**. This train was finished in LMS lake with gold stripes and is depicted below on its trial run at **Willesden** behind '6220', shortly before shipping to America. The Second World War prevented the train entering service as such in this country and although sufficient coaches (except two kitchen cars) were eventually built for three new trains the service was never revived after hostilities ceased.

Local passenger services of the later 1930s still exhibited considerable variety, although standard equipment was gradually coming into wider use. At the head of this page, the picture shows Stanier Jubilee No. 5718 **Dreadnought** ascending **Standish bank** near Wigan with a train of ex-LNWR coaches circa 1937–8. The locomotive is exhibiting the sans-serif style of insignia adopted for a short period during 1936–7 and was one of the many Jubilees to be paired with a Fowler tender. Note that in spite of the late date, the coaches still carry the fully lined livery.

The second picture shows a characteristic outer suburban train on the ex-LNWR main line heading north through **Tring cutting** behind Watford based Class 4P 2–6–4T No. 2489 circa 1938–9. The main portion of the train is a five coach set of fully panelled LMS standard coaches of 1927–8 vintage and it is strengthened at the rear by two third class coaches of later design. All the coaches are orthodox suburban third class types except for the third vehicle which is a full first with lavatory accommodation.

The bottom picture shows a push-pull train consisting of a pair of brake ended ex-LYR centre corridor types, the nearer vehicle being of 1910 vintage, the further one some ten years older. Worthy of mention is the characteristic LYR inward taper of the sides of the nearer coach to enable the guard to see forward along the train and yet dispense with the need for projecting lookouts. The coaches started life as main line vehicles before conversion for motor train working. Note the lack of end gangway and the fact that the coaches display the simplified livery adopted from 1934 onwards.

The changeover to standard stock seemed to take longer in Scotland than south of the border—in fact, several displaced coaches of English pre-group origin migrated north of the Border. Typical of the Scottish scene during the 1930s are the pictures on this page.

In the upper picture, Stanier Class 5 No. 5171 is seen leaving **Perth** with a southbound Aberdeen–Glasgow express in July 1939. The locomotive, unusually for a Class 5, displays the smallest LMS cabside numerals, which were widely used in Scotland during the late 1930s and early 1940s. The train is a mixture of LMS standard and pre-group stock. Particularly interesting is the leading vehicle which is an ex-Pullman dining car in LMS livery. The Caledonian had operated Pullman diners before the grouping but it was not until 1933 that the cars were purchased by the LMS.

The next view shows ex-HR Drummond 0–4–4T No. 15054 (ex-HR 46) waiting at **The Mound** with a mixed train for the Dornoch branch. The three coaches, all six wheel, are of MR, LNWR and GSWR origin respectively ! Elsewhere on the Highland section, equally distinctive vehicles were to be seen and the last picture, taken at **Aberfeldy** in August 1939, shows a somewhat unusual pair of coaches operating on the ex-HR branch from Ballinluig. The leading vehicle is an ex-MR double ended clerestory corridor brake (originally a 'slip' composite) and the second coach is an LMS standard wood panelled corridor composite brake of 1930 period. Shortly after this picture was taken, the LMS standard coach was rebuilt with Stanier pattern side panels. The locomotive is an ex-Caledonian Railway Drummond 0–6–0 No. 17415 (ex-CR 748).

The McIntosh 0–4–4Ts of the Caledonian Railway were robust and long lived engines. Most of them survived Nationalisation and here one sees two of them in local passenger service during late LMS/early BR days.

At the head of the page, No. 15230 (ex-CR 163) is seen passing **Camperdown Junction** on the Dundee and Arbroath joint line in June 1948 with a two coach local of early LMS standard stock. Below, No. 15130 (ex-CR 97) was photographed at **Marley Junction** in the West Riding during late LMS days with a two coach Keighley to Bradford local at a time when several of the ex-Caley tanks were operating in the West Riding. Note the rather unbecoming replacement stovepipe chimney. The leading coach of the train is an early LMS standard lavatory composite and the brake third is a Stanier vehicle.

By the close of the LMS period, gang-wayed stock was becoming increasingly common on longer distance stopping trains. Two North Country examples conclude this survey of LMS passenger trains.

Above, ex-MR Class 4P Compound 4–4–0 No. 1022, in austere black livery, is seen leaving **Skipton** in December 1946 with a four coach local composed entirely of Stanier corridor stock. The first coach is unlined—the normal wartime method for repainting carriage stock.

In early BR days, trains, like their early LMS forebears, showed little change except for livery and the lower view, taken at **Ais Gill** in the early 1950s, shows a formation absolutely typical of late LMS practice. The train is a Carlisle–Hellifield local behind Stanier Class 5 No. 44729. The leading coach is an early wood panelled LMS standard corridor brake composite, the centre vehicle is a Stanier period corridor composite and the rear vehicle is an 'all steel' corridor brake third or intermediate style (1931).

Featuring the 4F

'When in doubt, use a Class 4', seems to have been the philosophy of many operating areas of the LMS and, indeed, the 4F was a very versatile animal! Although finally out-numbered by the Stanier Class 5 in BR days, the Class 4 was numerically, the largest single class of locomotives on the LMS and for much of the lifetime of the company, was truly its 'maid of all work'.

There were 772 Class 4s. The Midland had built 192, the LMS added 575 after the grouping and in 1930, five more of MR type were acquired from the Somerset and Dorset. True, they were all the same basic locomotive, but to say they were all alike is somewhat akin to stating that all human beings have two legs! Nine variants are shown in this small selection alone but very many more permutations were possible. Basically, the ex-MR and S&D engines were right hand drive whereas most (but not all) of the LMS built machines were left hand drive. The pre-group engines were usually paired with Johnson style tenders with flared copings and coal rails while the LMS locomotives usually had Fowler tenders with straight side sheets, sometimes with additional coal rails. There were, however, many subsequent exchanges of tenders and when it came to chimneys and other ancillary details, no rules were followed.

The odd thing is that the 4F was not a particularly inspired design from the mechanical point of view—in fact it had many faults. But then, so had many other steam engines; but this never seemed to prevent most of them from gaining a real position of affection in the minds of the men who handled them—ask the driver of a 'Super D'! Sworn *by* in many places, sworn *at* in not a few others, the 4F was, nevertheless, as LMS as Lord Stamp!

The classic Midland 4F in a classic Midland setting (below). No. 3887 is seen heading south past the original North Midland station at **Ambergate** with a Rowsley to Derby limestone train. Note the Johnson pattern tender, Midland dome and tall Fowler chimney.

D

In the adjoining picture, ex-MR No. 3978 is seen near **Preston** with a down Blackpool excursion shortly after the grouping. The engine is coupled to the final style of MR flared top tender (with riveted side panels and no beading strips) and the locomotive, with its Ramsbottom safety valves, is in original MR condition. The train is a truly cosmopolitan affair. The leading vehicle is a Clayton ex-MR 48ft clerestory non-corridor lavatory composite brake, followed by an ex-MR Bain 54ft corridor third. Two assorted LNWR corridors and two more ex-MR coaches complete the first section of the train. At the very rear, some six-wheelers are present.

The second picture shows ex-MR No. 3987 at **Marley Junction**, Yorkshire, fairly late in LMS days. The engine has a replacement Stanier chimney and LMS dome. The tender is the same type as in the previous picture but the original beaded centre splasher on the engine has been replaced by a plain one.

The LMS built Class 4Fs had plain, not beaded splashers. The lower picture shows early LMS built No. 4040 in the late 1930s. It has, however, been modified to have an exhaust steam injector below the footplate. It has a new tall pattern Stanier chimney and the tail rod housings have been removed. This was a right hand drive engine and, although LMS built, was fitted when new with the second hand ex-Midland tender seen in this picture.

50

No. 4027 was the pioneer LMS standard 4F and is seen here, shortly after the grouping, with a train of ex-MR six wheelers on a Tilbury line train to St. Pancras. Amongst the detail differences from the ex-MR engines were the slightly less tall dome and chimney. These lower height fittings were adopted to give the LMS built engines greater route availability than the ex-MR version. The tender is of Fowler standard design.

The adjoining picture shows what might be termed the basic LMS Class 4 at the head of a mineral train. The locomotive is No. 4384 and is seen descending **Grayrigg** with a train of loaded wooden sided coke hoppers of NER origin. They were probably working to the Cumberland coast having joined the main line at Tebay from the LNER route over Stainmore. The locomotive is almost identical to that of the previous picture except for being left hand drive.

Express freight came as grist to the mill for the 4Fs and this picture shows LMS standard No. 4433 on a train consisting mostly of vans on the Midland main line. This particular 4F had a tall Fowler chimney like the Midland built engines but it still had the lower profile LMS dome.

Three LMS standard Class 4s in widely differing locations and on widely different duties complete this study of the familiar LMS workhorse.

Above is No. 4418 specially posing on a newly built train of high capacity coal hoppers at **Trent** on 15th October 1929. The locomotive is in pre-1928 livery. At a much later date (7th June 1939), No. 4445 had lost its tail rod housings, had been fitted with a replacement Stanier chimney and was coupled to a Fowler tender with coal rails when photographed at **Berkhamsted** with a Broad Street to Tring local.

Finally, Hellifield based No. 4555 was rostered to **a** Leeds—Morecambe residential train when seen passing **Steeton** (below) in late LMS days. Note the plates fixed to the buffer beam where the tail rod housings had been removed.

By Tilbury to Southend

For some time after the grouping, the familiar 4–4–2 Tilbury tanks, together with their sets of pre-grouping coaches, continued to run most of the services on the London, Tilbury and Southend line much as they had always done. The fact that the LMS continued to build Tilbury tanks, saw fit to provide special sets of coaches for the trains and, in later days, virtually confined the 3-cylinder Stanier 2–6–4Ts to this area, can only have fostered the impression that the Tilbury was, somehow, different from the rest of the system—which, of course, it was! Indeed, there always seemed to be something slightly improper about the way in which the LMS, by virtue of its ownership of the Tilbury line, had obtained for itself such a considerable slice of the commuter pie of southern East Anglia!

Almost totally cut off from the rest of its parent system, the Tilbury had a character all its own and its semi-isolation only served to reinforce the distinctive characteristics which were already well marked long before the Midland Railway took it over in 1912 and which were hardly less in evidence at the grouping. For the Midland, although painting the engines red, had left most of the coaches in their original teak finish. The LMS, on the other hand, as if, perhaps, to re-assure itself that it really did own this compact redoubt in the heart of LNER territory, painted red almost everything in sight during the first few post-grouping years. But this never seemed to make much difference and the Tilbury continued to be the Tilbury!

Perhaps it was because it was that rare species amongst British railways—a passenger line. One always felt that though goods traffic might be the bread and butter trade for most of the LMS, it was regarded on the Tilbury lines as something one did not discuss in the best circles.

The main line from Fenchurch Street to Southend and Shoeburyness ran via Tilbury but there was also a cut-off route from Barking to Pitsea, by-passing Tilbury, which ran via Upminster and on which most of the through traffic to Southend was operated. One should not, however, forget the considerable boat train traffic to and from Tilbury docks and the cross-river passenger ferry from Tilbury to Gravesend which gave the LMS a station right in the heart of the Southern Railway parish.

To the LMS, the Tilbury was almost, in a geographical sense, what the GNSR was to the LNER. There can be few doubts as to who had the better bargain!

The 'LMS look' on the Tilbury is well portrayed by this view of Stanier Class 4P 3-cylinder 2–6–4T No. 2536 leaving **Fenchurch Street** with the 4.56 p.m. train to Southend in 1939. The locomotive was based at Shoeburyness and the train is an LMS standard 11 coach set of fully panelled 54ft non-corridor stock, specially built for the Tilbury line. It will be noted that the engine carries express passenger head-lamps and is routed via the Upminster cut-off.

The Tilbury line trains were generally much tidier in appearance than those on most other LMS lines. This was because the coaches had, traditionally, always been delivered as set formations of matching stock which tended to remain unchanged during most of their life.

In the upper picture, a very early set of ex-LT & SR four-wheelers is seen shortly after grouping headed by ex-LT & SR Whitelegg 4–4–2T No. 2125 (ex-LT & SR No. 16 **Low Street**). This type of engine was the smallest of the Tilbury tank designs and dated from 1880. Driving wheel diameter was 6ft 0in and the type was classified 1P by the LMS. During 1927, this engine was renumbered firstly to 2190 and, later, to 2067 to make room for the construction of new 4–4–2Ts.

One of these newer engines, LMS 2119, is seen in the second picture at the head of a train of fairly late design LT & SR bogie coaches. Delivered in 1923 to an ex-MR order, the engine was basically identical to the final Tilbury tank design of 1905 which was, in turn, derived from the class depicted in the bottom picture. The LMS eventually built 35 of these 'ultimate' Tilbury tanks to add to the 16 pre-group examples which it had inherited and of which the preserved **Thundersley** is one. The LMS classified the engines 3P and they had 6ft 9in driving wheels.

The intermediate design of Tilbury tank is shown in the final picture. LMS No. 2170 started life as LT & SR No. 63 **Mansion House**, a Whitelegg design of 1900. Classified 2P by the LMS, it had 6ft 9in driving wheels and was renumbered to 2104 in 1927/8. The mammoth 13 coach set is of high roofed Midland Railway design. Like their LMS descendants, these coaches were built specially for the Tilbury line services.

Some trains on the Tilbury were slightly less standardised and two such formations are shown on this page. There is another example on page 51. Above is shown a through train to St. Pancras passing **Leigh on Sea** on 22nd August 1936. These services diverged from the main Tilbury route at Barking East Junction and gained access to St. Pancras via the Tottenham and Forest Gate and the Tottenham and Hampstead joint lines. The locomotive is Stanier Class 5 No. 5053 of Kentish Town shed and the train is mostly composed of ex-MR low roofed non-corridor stock but with a gangwayed full brake at the front and an ex-MR clerestory at the rear.

The lower picture shows a rarely photographed double headed combination of two Stanier 3-cylinder 2–6–4Ts, 2527 and 2534, coupled bunker to bunker and seen approaching **Southend**, also on 22nd August 1936. The train is mainly ex-LT & SR bogie stock but with an ex-MR clerestory as the leading vehicle.

CATHERINE
LONDON

A less well documented feature associated with the Tilbury line was the Tilbury–Gravesend passenger ferry. Opposite (above) is shown **Tilbury Riverside** station. The first such station at Tilbury dated from 1854 when the cross-river steam ferry service was initiated; but the station illustrated was constructed in accordance with the 1921 agreement with the Port of London Authority. It was opened by Ramsay Macdonald on 16th May 1930. The landing stage, which rose and fell with the tide, was 1142ft long of which the LMS owned 300ft for ferry traffic. The rest of the frontage, seen in the distance, was used for ocean liner traffic.

The ferry boat shown in the upper picture is the S.S. **Edith**, built in 1911 by A. W. Robertson and Co. Ltd., of London. She was 283 tons gross, 136ft long by 37ft beam and drew 5ft 3in of water. Fitted with a four-cylinder coal fired compound steam engine she could carry 850 passengers at a maximum speed of nine knots. She was withdrawn for scrap in 1961.

S.S. **Catherine** (opposite, below), was a smaller boat of 259 tons built in 1903 by the same firm. She could carry 648 passengers and was 129ft long by 32ft 6in beam with a 5ft draught. Also coal fired, S.S. 'Catherine' was withdrawn in late 1960.

The picture on this page shows the other end of the ferry service—the LMS ferry station at **Gravesend**—during pre-war days. When the Gravesend road vehicle ferry service was closed in 1965, foot passengers transferred to the old road vehicle terminal at Gravesend, thus enabling the ex-LMS station to be closed.

Not the conventional approach to the High Peak but, nevertheless, an interesting one. These pictures, taken on 10th October 1951, show ex-MR Class 3F 0–6–0 No. 43763 of Derby shed, with an ex-MR goods-brake, shunting at **Wirksworth**. The far track behind the shed was the short branch line from the Steeplehouse direction which lies away to the left of the area shown in the picture. On the day these pictures were taken, 43763 seems to have been shunting a train which had come from Steeplehouse and this can just be discerned in the distance in the second picture.

Perhaps the most surprising feature of this almost 19th Century scene at **Cromford Wharf** (above), is the fact that the LMS apparently saw fit to grace it with one of their latest enamel trespass boards. It is just visible to the right of the signal post—partly obscured by the swirling smoke of an unseen locomotive.

Below is shown a portion of the original Cromford and High Peak fishbelly rail at Cromford Wharf.

From the Midland to the high peak

Amongst the spider's web of lines woven by the Midland Railway in and around the Peak District, there was a charming little branch line which left the Derby–Manchester main line at Duffield and wended its way to the settlement of Wirksworth where it terminated—at least to all outward appearances. However, sneaking away round the back of the locomotive shed at Wirksworth, almost as though it was slightly ashamed of itself, what appeared to be just another siding disappeared from view beneath the overbridge.

The casual visitor could be pardoned if he thought no more about the matter but the more curious were well rewarded if they followed this line, for it eventually arrived at Steeplehouse where there could be found a most unusual section of the LMS, the Cromford and High Peak Railway.

The High Peak line was one of the oldest to come into the LMS group, its origins being contemporary with those of the Liverpool and Manchester Railway. Originally 33 miles long connecting Cromford and Whaley Bridge, it had been extensively modified by the LNWR (its eventual owners) and, in places, closed well before the grouping. By the time the LMS was formed, only the section between Cromford and Parsley Hay remained substantially as its designer had intended.

It was in the mode of operation that the High Peak line was most distinctive. In a sense it was built rather like a canal with (fairly) level sections interspersed with formidable inclines. Many of the latter were too steep to be worked by conventional means and cable haulage was adopted. However, amongst the less steep inclines (!), that at Hopton *was* worked in later days by conventional means and provided some spectacular pyrotechnics over the years as a variety of small tank engines pounded up the steepest gradient to be worked by adhesion on the LMS. The final pitch was at 1 in 14 but only after successive stretches at 1 in 60, 1 in 30 and 1 in 20 !

As far as is known, LMS standard engines did not work the line particularly regularly. The nearest were probably some BR built derivatives of the Stanier 0–4–0STs, but the last locomotives of LMS constituent origin were the 0–6–0Ts which had started life in the very different surroundings of the North London Railway (later part of the LNWR). Although the Cromford and High Peak line is no more, one of its NLR tank engines is, happily, preserved on the Bluebell Railway. Sheffield Park is no Middleton Top but some visitors will remember. . . .

Middleton Incline—top and bottom. This rope-worked section was situated between Steeple-house and Hopton, its gradient was 1 in 8½ and it rose 253 feet in a distance of 2124 feet. Behind the almost ecclesiastical outline of the winding house at the top of the incline was located the shed which housed the locomotives which worked up the Hopton incline. The two vehicles shown on the right hand track of the upper picture were used to carry water from Cromford to Middleton Top for both locomotive and domestic use. They were built on the frames of old LNWR tenders. After arrival at the top, the water was discharged from the tank trucks to a pit and thence by a pipe to a reservoir which fed both the stationary winding engine and the locomotives.

Middleton Top was the last regular home for several ex-NLR 0–6–0Ts. One of them, BR 58860 (ex-NLR No. 92; LNWR No. 2892; LMS No. 7527, later 27527) is seen outside the engine shed on 5th June 1950, prior to heading a special working of water tanks up the Hopton incline. Such was the precious nature of water in these limestone hills that even the rain-water falling on the shed roof was drained off by downspout into the reservoir.

Later in the same day in 1950, 58860 is seen attacking the final part of the **Hopton** incline with its special train (above). Note the gradient board reading 1 in 20/1 in 14.

The stretch of line from Hopton Top to Parsley Hay was, by Cromford and High Peak standards, a fairly conventional piece of railway, although it contained some fearsome curves. In the picture below, a mixed freight is seen at **Longcliffe** heading in the direction of Parsley Hay. Appropriately enough, a typical ex-LNWR brake van brings up the rear of the train.

Above is shown the LMS Royal Train made up for a day journey from Euston to Edinburgh circa 1934. The locomotive is Royal Scot No. 6127 **Old Contemptibles**. The ten coach formation contains the two Royal Saloons, two brake firsts, two dining cars and three semi-Royal saloons plus an unidentified coach next to the rear end brake. The LMS did not maintain a special Royal Train locomotive but the train was usually hauled on the main lines by the latest express type in service. Below, the overnight Royal Train from Ballater to Euston is seen passing **Kilburn High Road** at 7.50 a.m. on 18th October 1938 behind blue streamlined Stanier 4–6–2 No. 6221 **Queen Elizabeth**. Note the addition of sleeping cars (behind the leading brake) to the formation.

For King and Country

In an age when to be proud of being British is not infrequently regarded with suspicion, it is pleasing to be able to record that the railway service has always been amongst the most patriotic of institutions to be found in the land. Nowhere has this been more apparent than in the efforts made to ensure the safety and comfort of the Sovereign when he or she chooses to travel by rail. During the particular circumstances of the second world war, it was scarcely less an honour to have the safe custody of the Prime Minister in one's hands. To the LMS fell the distinction of providing trains for both these purposes and while other companies also had their Royal and VIP trains, it is fair to claim that the LMS facilities were used considerably more frequently than those of the other British railway systems.

Until 1941, the LMS Royal Train was entirely composed of the beautiful vehicles built at Wolverton works by the LNWR, the most impressive coaches being, of course, the two twelve-wheel saloons built in 1903/4 for King Edward VII and Queen Alexandra. By request of King George V the train retained its LNWR livery at the grouping but at the outbreak of war, it was repainted in LMS crimson lake to make it less conspicuous. In addition to the two Royal saloons, there were also available for the train no fewer than six semi-Royal saloons of matching style but on four-wheel bogies, together with two converted ex-LNWR corridor first class brakes. Sleeping and dining cars completed the formation and these cars were of basically LNWR type, again of the twelve-wheel pattern. There were also one or two other special saloons if needed. It was rare that the full complement of saloons was rostered to the train since much depended on the nature of the journey and the size of the entourage. However, the train generally carried at least one dining car and a few semi-Royals in addition to the main saloons and the brake ends. Sleeping cars were, of course, confined to overnight trips. Most coaches were of classical LNWR clerestory style and, fortunately, both the Royal saloons and two of the dining cars have been preserved.

In 1941, with the building of two new armour plated Royal saloons there began the gradual replacement of the old LNWR stock with more modern vehicles. However, one or two pre-group coaches still remained in use in 1970.

It was not until World War II that it was felt necessary to assemble a special train for Prime Ministerial use. The train was formed from LMS vehicles and saw service in all parts of the country. Most of the coaches were of LMS standard design but two of the ex-LNWR semi-Royal saloons, being surplus to immediate requirements, were adapted for the personal use of Mr. Churchill. Naturally, it being wartime, the train, like the Royal train, was operated under conditions of extreme security and no pictures have been located of it in service. Indeed, the only known official picture is one featured below and this was not taken until after hostilities ceased. From the left hand end, the coaches in the formation were as follows: corridor brake composite; composite sleeping car; kitchen car; first class open dining car; two ex-LNWR semi-Royal saloons; first class sleeping car; corridor brake first.

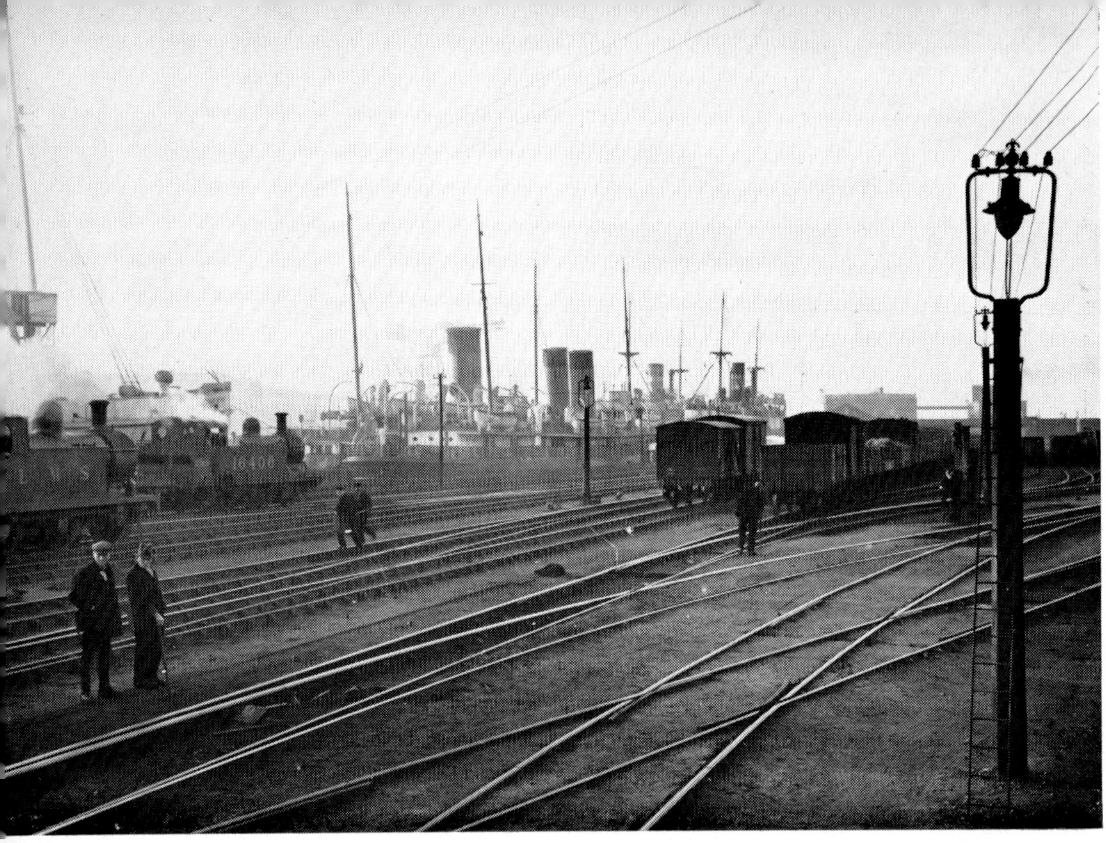
16400

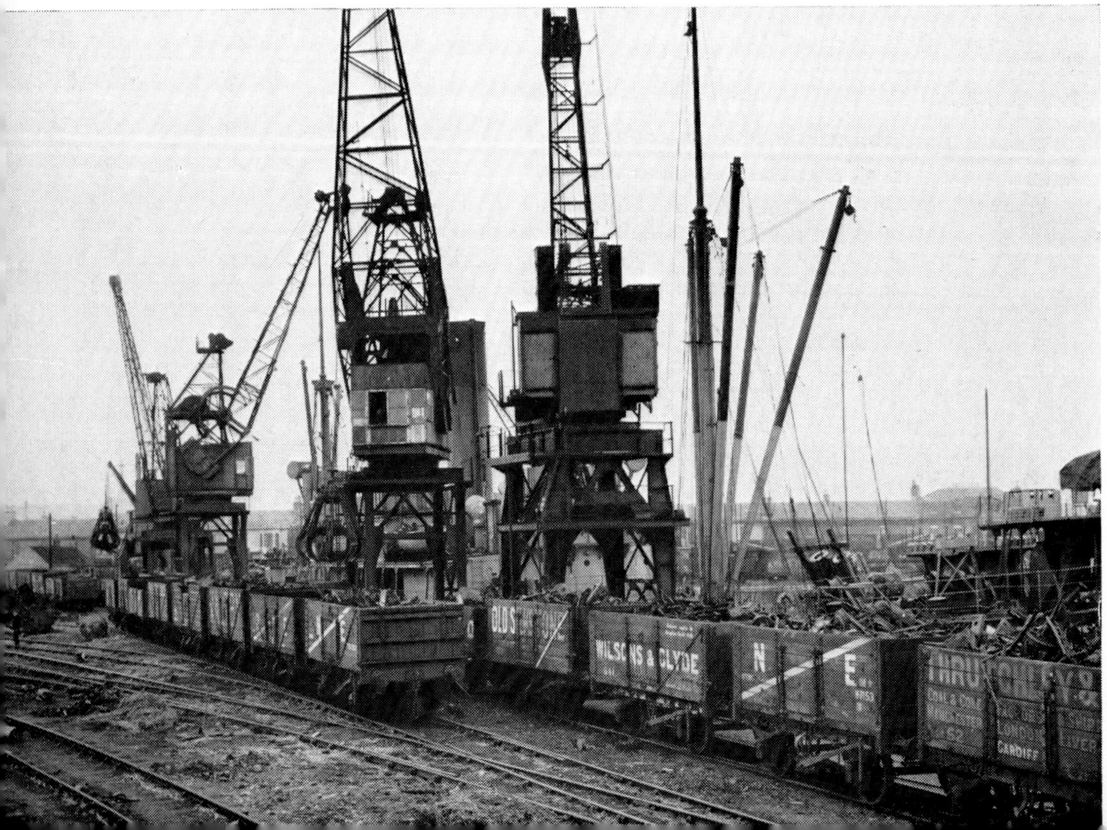
WILSONS & CLYDE
CARDIFF

Docks and harbours

The involvement of the LMS in maritime affairs ranged from the ownership and operation of sea going ships to the running of pleasure cruises on the English lakes. But as well as operating its own vessels, the LMS also carried massive quantities of freight to the many ports where it had marshalling yards.

Opposite (above) is seen a portion of the marshalling yards at **Barrow-in-Furness** *circa* 1930. Seen shunting are LMS standard class 3F 0–6–0T No. 16406 (later 7323) and an ex-Furness Railway 0–6–0T. Alongside the quay, laid up for winter, are the Isle of Man Steam Packet Company's vessels **Mona's Queen** and **Mona's Isle**. This was a spacious yard, by contrast with the rather congested conditions at **Ardrossan** (opposite, below) where a consignment of scrap iron is being handled. Ardrossan was also the embarkation point for the ex-CR and ex-GSWR steamer services to the Isle of Arran.

Garston Dock, just south of Liverpool on the north bank of the Mersey estuary was not as well known as some other coastal locations. However, its traffic was not unimportant and in the picture to the right, above, a load of pit props is being transferred to railway wagons.

At centre right, the LMS packet steamer **Duke of Rothesay** is seen leaving **Heysham Harbour** bound for Belfast. This ship, along with its two sisters, inaugurated the improved LMS service from Heysham to Belfast in 1928. The ship was capable of carrying 1500 passengers (400 in sleeping berths) and its 66,000 cu ft hold space could cope, amongst other things, with 300 head of cattle. There were also stalls for eight racehorses.

By complete contrast with these mainly commercial scenes, the view of **Bowness Pier** on lake Windermere in pre-war days (below), recalls more relaxing times afloat. Bowness is just about halfway along Lake Windermere between the ex-Furness terminus of Lakeside at the south end and Ambleside at the northern end of the lake. During the summer months, frequent pleasure boat trips were made between all three points. In this picture, ex-Furness Railway steam yacht **Cygnet** is just about to leave the pier.

In the picture above, ex-MR 0–10–0 No. 2290, together with no fewer than three Class 3F 0–6–0Ts is seen banking a heavy northbound freight. Below, in a specially posed picture, the headlamp of 2290 is demonstrated being focussed on an ex-MR goods brake at about the time of the grouping.

Bromsgrove to New Street

Bromsgrove to New Street—what memories those place names revive . . . miles apart with scarcely a level yard between and at both ends of the line the pilot engines. Ah yes, the pilot engines!

At Bromsgrove lived the unique 0—10—0 with its bevy of small 0—6—0Ts; while at New Street stood a solitary (and rather elderly) 4—4—0, its smokebox pointing west, ready to assist westbound passenger trains. The contrast in duties was equally marked. 'Big Emma' and her legions would pound away all day and all night at the rear of northbound trains as they climbed the Lickey but the New Street West Pilot, to give it the full grandiose title, seemed to live most of its life more in hope than expectation as it stood, burning coal, just waiting and hoping. Occasionally it would timidly venture out to do a spot of surreptitious shunting in the fish bays but most of the time it lived a very sheltered life! Sometimes, however, came the odd few hours of glory when the West Pilot was called upon to greater service than shunting vans or pushing westbound passenger trains as far as Church Road Junction. On these red letter days she might even have found herself on the *front* of the train destined, perhaps, to try and help the train engine all the way to Gloucester—adventure indeed! Mark you, it was sometimes debatable whether the West Pilot ever achieved more than to be pushed along at rather indecent speed by the somewhat more lively 5X coupled to the train itself!

However, the story of Bromsgrove to New Street is really the story of the Lickey Incline and we have chosen to tell it from the fireman's point of view. Lest we be accused of inventing the tale, we must hasten to point out that it is a true story and, we believe, probably unique amongst the annals of this famous route. The fireman was one Terry Essery, the younger brother of one of the authors:

The Fireman's Tale

"The greatest sustained effort Tom made with any engine whilst in my company was, without doubt, the run from Gloucester to Birmingham with the Bristol–Sheffield Night Mail. We Saltley men only worked the job on Sunday mornings, maybe because it was routed the 'hard way'—via Worcester! As far as I can recall, we were due to relieve a Bristol crew at about 2.50 a.m. on Gloucester station. However, on this particular occasion, it was something like 3.05 a.m. when 5699 'Galatea' trundled in with no less than 14 coaches behind the tender.

"Even in the dim platform lighting we noticed to our joy the gleaming paint-work of a recent shopping. 'She's a beauty—steams like a kettle even with the dampers shut' were the only words the Bristol fireman said—and she was.

The New Street West Pilot. Ex-MR Class 2P 4—4—0 No. 369 is seen here at New Street on West Pilot duty during the 1930s. No. 369 was a Deeley non-super heated rebuild of an original Johnson design.

Galatea herself in the late 1930s, some ten years before her mighty exploits recounted on this page.

After putting the 'bag' into the tank I had a quick look at the coal. Here again I was pleased to find that it was topped up with best quality hard coal, well broken and neatly trimmed—so far so good. A glance in the firebox showed a perfect fire—nicely burnt through, correct shape and no holes. Everything was adding up to ideal conditions for an extraordinary run. A freshly shopped 5X in superb condition, a heavy load, grade one coal, a perfect fire, Tom and I wishing to get home as soon as possible and a late start thrown in for good measure. Just how extraordinary the run was to be I did not imagine at that stage. Although I had been with Tom long enough to be well used to his methods, we had never worked a 5X together.

"Out with the bag, ten quick shovelsful round the box and we were right away.

"Tom eased her out of the platform while I busied myself with sighting the 'pegs' which were visible first on my side. 'O.K. Tom, we've got the back 'un.' The blast sharpened and that beautiful double three beat which only the 5X plays with such virtuosity sounded like music in my ears as I bent to flash another 'quick ten' round the box.

"The run to Cheltenham was not spectacular due to the numerous permanent way restrictions in operation. However, it did serve to prove what a magnificent piece of machinery 'Galatea' was. Here was the impression of titanic power straining at the leash and I felt confident that between us we could answer almost any demand that even Tom might make. Having to 'draw up' at Cheltenham caused further delay but finally the whistle blew and we were off at last.

"A brief half slip and 'Galatea' quickly accelerated her 420 odd tons load out of the platform, her blast crashing out into the still night air. Tom was determined to 'pull a bit back' but it was not to be—just yet! 'Galatea' was getting into her stride—and what a wonderful stride it was; her 6ft 9in drivers turning so smoothly that one might have been in a first class dining car—no knocks, no rattles, no violent lurching. 'Why can't they all be like this?'

" 'Back 'uns on!'—a quiet oath from Tom meant that he too had seen the distant at caution. Since we were running late, a fitted freight had been turned out in front of us and we had caught it up.

"At Worcester I prepared for the coming onslaught. Slick work by the GPO saved a few minutes and, knowing Tom, this was where the effort would start to be made. Without so much as a shudder 5699 surged forward, seemingly as determined as Tom. Out of the tunnel she stormed, her double three beat rising to an even crisper note as the pace quickened through Blackpole and on to Droitwich—no signal checks this time. Out through that sleepy little spa town we blasted—ever climbing, ever accelerating. The individual beats had almost mingled to a continuous roar now—'It's a wonder it doesn't blow the chimney

68

off!' A quick glance to assure myself of its existence and there on the top of the smokebox was what appeared to be a miniature volcano at full throttle. Despite the thickness of fire which I had managed to maintain, an almost continual stream of blazing coal and cinders was being hurled high into the air by this enormous blast and the sparks could be seen bouncing off even the last of our 14 coaches. The whole countryside was illuminated by this immense firework display, the like of which I had never seen before. 'Galatea' certainly had the bit between her teeth now.

"Despite this hammering, the needle never left the red line and so great was the evaporation rate that the exhaust injector would not maintain the water level in the boiler and I was obliged to supplement this with bursts from the live steam injector. I was now being kept pretty busy. The tender doors had been open some time and a number of lumps were requiring the attention of the coal pick between bouts of almost continual shovelling. I was, therefore, thankful for the brief respite offered by our stop for bankers at Bromsgrove. This was my last chance to make sure that everything was in order for our assault on the bank. With both injectors singing away, topping up the boiler and just keeping the safety valves closed, I was able to make my final preparations to the fire. A few carefully placed shovelsful levelled the bed, preventing any tendency for holes to be dragged in that great incandescent mass.

"The $2\frac{1}{4}$ miles of 1 in 37 that constitutes the Lickey incline has set the scene for many a famous tale—but few were as spectacular as the happenings of the next seven minutes or so. The two Class 3F bankers had rolled into position and I leaned out of the window, regaining my breath and at the same time listening for that distinctive whistle. There it was, clear and shrill in the night air. Before the echoes had died away, 'Galatea' bellowed her reply and Tom had the regulator open. Both injectors off and a quick look astern to see that all was well. A column of sparks indicated that at least one of the bankers was trying hard. Acceleration

A typical Lickey Scene. Hughes/Fowler 'Crab' Class 2–6–0 No. 2763 was seen on the bank on 29th May 1935 banked by 0–10–0 No. 2290. The train is a mixture of David Bain ex-MR and pre-Stanier LMS standard stock.

over the first few yards through the station before we hit the bank proper was impressive and then as we started to climb, 5699 settled to a steady ponderous beat. With exhaust injector on, I once again took up the shovel. The regulator was now wide open but I was happy in the knowledge that the pressure was steady on the 225 lbs per square inch mark. Half way up the bank, 'Galatea' was incredibly smooth on a 50% cut-off, showing no signs of shortness of breath and was, if anything, gaining time. Then, without warning, she checked in her stride as if some giant hand was dragging her back. Tom uttered a few more oaths of vaguely nautical origin which, loosely translated, meant that he did not think the bankers were doing a fat lot now! (Indeed they were not for, we subsequently learned, the leading banker's fireman, while commendably enthusiastic, was still very inexperienced and had filled the boiler to such a degree as to cause excessive priming. This, apart from obliging the driver to shut the regulator, also caused the ejectors to fail which consequently applied the brakes. Despite rapid action by the driver, the 14 coach train 'left' the bankers and it is to the driver's lasting credit that he was able under such difficult circumstances to once again take position at the rear of the train without so much as a shudder being felt. Unfortunately, the priming was so bad that we had almost reached Blackwell before he was again able to do any useful work).

"It was against Tom's nature to moan about other people's shortcomings. If the bankers were not doing their stuff then we would have to do a bit more. A lesser driver than Tom would have sat down on the bank to wait for the bankers to start again. A lesser engine that 'Galatea' would have given him no choice but Tom knew his locomotive and without further ado he wound the gear down to the full forward position of 75% cut-off. She responded like a thoroughbred. The exhaust crashed out in a unbelievable volume of sound reverberating across the hills like a thunderclap—'Galatea' had the lot!

"Imperceptibly at first, but increasing all the time, her great pulse quickened. The impossible was happening before my very eyes. 'Galatea' was actually accelerating this huge load of 420 tons up Bromsgrove Bank without the aid of banking engines! The sight and sound of this great beast at full song inspired me to redouble my own efforts, and I was already working like a demon gone mad, but the reward was on the pressure gauge and the boiler was as full as it should be.

"With Blackwell in sight, 5699 seemed to gallop forward in a triumphant blast of energy. Twin columns of sparks from the rear showed that the bankers were trying desperately to make up for their mid-bank lapse. We caught a fleeting glimpse of unlit platforms and a through freight waiting to descend and then we were away and heading for Barnt Green with the bankers already far behind.

"As the gradient levelled off, so Tom wound back the screw but our speed had now increased to the point where single exhaust beats were scarcely discernible and an ever increasing column of fire was rocketing from our chimney. I went over to Tom and glanced at the gear indicator—45%. Seeing me do this, he looked up enquiringly: 'She O.K. at that?' I bellowed my consent, adding with what I thought was thinly veiled sarcasm, 'In fact, I should drop her down another half turn.' He did!

"Past Barnt Green and the gradient with us, the acceleration was fantastic. The continuous jet of fire now erupting from our chimney was cascading along the full length of the train floodlighting our progress like some gigantic phantom from the underworld. I had built up an immense fire while climbing the bank and had continued firing until approaching Barnt Green. The majority of express drivers shut off at the road bridge just beyond Halesowen Junction Signal Box (provided, of course, they have had an unchecked run from Blackwell) and from here on they coast down through Northfield along to the curve at Kings Norton where speed has to be checked down to 35 m.p.h. I calculated that even con-suming fuel at that terrific rate, 'Galatea' had more than enough in the box to last until shut off point. It was just as well because Tom was certainly not one of the majority of drivers.

"As we thundered down through the cutting towards Halesowen Junction, I made no attempt to fire the engine. The mere act of opening the doors would have admitted too much cold air and although the water level was down to little more than half a glass, the needle was still on that red line. Tom made no move to close the regulator as we raced past the road bridge. The distant for Northfield loomed up and still no movement from Tom. I decided to dispense with the exhaust injector for a few moments—I wanted to maintain full pressure until the end and surely he would shut off soon.

"Galatea's' exhaust had by now risen to a terrible ferocity, the individual beats having long since merged into a continual thunderous roar. Never before had I heard such a vast cacaphony of sound. She seemed to be tearing out her very heart and soul for us and a lump rose in my throat when I saw that the needle was *still* on the red line! How could she possibly stand up to this murderous treatment and still steam? It was incredible to think that the 5XPs were temperamental steamers when first introduced. The sight and sound of 5699 on that Sunday morning as we approached Northfield station is indelibly printed upon my mind. the exhilaration was indescribable.

"I caught a fleeting glimpse of the 'Bobby's' face pressed against the windows of Northfield box before it exploded in a blaze of fire. As the cascade of sparks cleared from the cab I looked back along the train. As far as the eye could see, a veritable blizzard of fire and flame swirled and danced and I recall wondering if the firebars themselves would be the next to go. Never before (or since) have I travelled through Northfield station at such a speed—but 'Galatea's' mighty effort was now nearly over. With a final tremendous blast we roared under the road bridge beyond the station to where the Kings Norton distants can be sighted. Three seconds afterwards and Tom slammed shut the regulator at the same time making a full brake application. This time the sparks came from the wheels! On with both injectors and a quick look at the fire—or, rather, what was left of it because there was only a thin layer of white hot cinders with the bars showing through in places. But at least it was clean!

"Back to the shovel and from Kings Norton I had the rare experience of firing in earnest as far as Five Ways. I say rare because normally the fireman can devote these last few minutes to cleaning down the footplate and making sure that everything is in apple pie order for the relief crew at New Street. On this occasion, it was a hard fight to keep enough fire in the box to get us to Five Ways.

"As the brake blocks released from the wheels on the last coach rounding Kings Norton Curve, so Tom heaved up the regulator to the horizontal again. 'Galatea' once more shattered the night air with her explosive roar, swaying majestically through those numerous bends from Bournville past Selly Oak to Five Ways, where she was at last allowed to coast down through the five tunnels into New Street. As she finally came to rest at the end of Platform 7, I found myself wondering what Tom might have done with a 4–6–2! However, the relief fireman's adverse comment regarding the amount of coal consumed brought me back to earth. Perhaps it was just as well that the 'Lizzies' did not run on our bit of track!

"I joined Tom as he rolled his way to the exit intent on catching the shed bus. He seemed well pleased at having pulled back so much time from Worcester. Meanwhile, the guard came running up, more than somewhat excited. We knew him well as a conscientious railwayman who enjoyed a sense of achievement when 'his' train made up time. 'Hey', he said, 'I've had the very dickens of a job with a young soldier who caused an almighty panic running down the train shouting that it was on fire and wanting to pull the cord. Took me all the way from Barnt Green to convince him that it was only sparks from the engine.' 'Mind You', he added in an aside to me, 'I thought you were chucking out a fair amount, but you know Tom.'

"Yes, I knew Tom. . . ."

Manifold motive power

E. R. Calthrop was engineer to the Leek and Manifold and he had been engineer to the Barsi Railway in India. Not surprisingly, the Manifold locomotives turned out to be almost identical to their Indian progenitors. Two engines only were built, complete with double roofed cabs, enormous headlamps and even bolt holes in the buffer beams for the non-existent cowcatchers!

They were 2–6–4Ts, the first of that wheel arrangement in Great Britain and identical except in odd details. The pictures show them both in their final LMS plain black livery—totally devoid of marks of ownership. Even at the end they were kept spotless as is clear from the appearance of No. 1 **E. R. Calthrop** as it stands alongside the coaling stage at **Hulme End**. They were big engines for narrow gauge machines and the bunker end view of No. 2 **J. B. Earle** shows off their fine proportions to good effect.

Farewell Manifold

At the grouping, the LMS paid £30,000 for the privilege of acquiring a debit balance of £14,000 and an annual loss of £2,000! Such were the harsh monetary facts of that most captivating narrow gauge line, the 2ft 6in gauge Leek and Manifold Valley Light Railway; and it is not surprising that it fell to the LMS to preside over its demise. Opened in 1904, one feels bound to think more in hope than expectation, the Manifold saw but 30 years of active life before, like so many others, it finally fell foul of the great gods 'Economy' and 'Internal Combustion'.

Perhaps it was too much to expect the LMS ever to take it seriously—the line had been a financial liability almost since its opening and the day of the narrow gauge tourist line was too far in the future. In fact, when one looks at the map and the distance of the stations from the nearest settlements, it was something of a miracle that the line survived as long as it did.

The LMS made, at best, only a half-hearted attempt to keep things going. For a few years, however, the two splendid engines were decked out in the full glory of the Crimson Lake livery and the carriages were similarly treated. However, the all pervading black eventually crept into Hulme End too and the end was not far away. The last public train ran on March 10th 1934, the line was dismantled in 1936 and Sir Josiah Stamp, President of the LMS Executive, declared it open in its new role as a public footpath in July 1937.

One cannot help feeling that it was all rather sad. Ill-conceived the line may have been but the motives of its founders were of the very highest and as a finished product, the railway had that indefinable something called 'style'. Even in the final drab livery, the engines possessed elegance and character. It was almost as if the resemblance of the Manifold's trains to those of the Barsi Light Railway of India had brought with it some of the timelessness of the Orient to the English hills.

So died the Manifold—its only known relics being the nameplates of its two engines and the headlamp of one of them. Farewell Manifold—you deserved a better fate.

The Manifold had only four passenger coaches but what splendid vehicles they were. There were two thirds (with verandahs at both ends) and two brake composites (with verandah at one end only), all being 42ft long by 8ft wide and 10ft high. They tared almost 13 tons each and special sanction from the Board of Trade was required to permit such large vehicles to run on 2ft 6in gauge. A rather charming feature of operations was that passengers could stand on the ornately decorated verandahs when the trains were in motion. All seats were cushioned and by all accounts, the coaches were as comfortable as they were stylish. The picture depicts a brake composite (LMS 14990) in fully lined livery standing at **Hulme End** in May 1934.

To avoid transhipment of loads, transporter cars were provided on which standard gauge wagons could be carried. At the point of changeover the standard gauge rails were set 10ins higher than the narrow gauge to enable the standard gauge rails to line up with the inverted channel iron which served as a rail on the transporter. This picture shows No. 1 **E. R. Calthrop** removing two 'United Dairies' glass lined milk tanks from **Ecton Creamery** on the first part of their journey to Finsbury Park. By the early 1930s, this daily milk service was the only stable factor in traffic receipts and the closure of the creamery in 1932 sounded the death knell for the Manifold.

The railway ran from Waterhouses to Hulme End. At **Waterhouses** it made a cross-platform interchange with the standard gauge North Staffordshire branch to Leek. The picture shows the narrow gauge platform with a typical Manifold train, alongside the station and with the ex-North Staffordshire standard gauge platform beyond the fence on the right. The vast number of platform trolleys was for the transhipment of milk churns from narrow to standard gauge vehicles.

Hulme End for Sheen and Hartington
(below). Here were coal and watering
facilities together with engine and goods
sheds. The view 'over the wall' shows the
entry to Hulme End station in LMS days
with a two coach set alongside the station—
a full third is nearer to the camera. Note the
absence of a conventional raised passenger
platform. The second picture, regrettably of
rather poor quality, is of chief interest in
depicting the one and only covered van
owned by the Leek and Manifold. It was of
steel construction, built by Leeds Forge and
it ran on Fox's patent steel frames and
bogies. Used often for milk churn traffic it
was Manifold No. 3, LMS No. 195316.
Note also the standard gauge wagons in the
background.

At the approach to **Waterhouses**, the
line passed the site of the original terminus
(above). On the opening day, triumphal
arches were erected across both road and
railway in the vicinity of the more distant
of the cottages in this view.

Signal boxes, old and new

For several years after the grouping, the four divisions of the LMS (Western, Central, Midland and Northern) pursued their appropriate pre-group signalling practices and it was some years before an overall company policy emerged. Even then, it was generally applied only when signals and other equipment became due for replacement. The signals themselves were resilient enough but when it came to signalboxes, there was scarcely ever an occasion for the LMS to deploy its standard design. In consequence, although standard LMS upper quadrant signals gradually became more widespread, the signalbox for the most part remained unchanged. As the years passed, the signalbox, more than almost any other item of company property, continued to reveal the original ownership of many stretches of line long after the locomotives and rolling stock had turned over to LMS standard types. Not surprisingly, therefore, this selection of pictures has something of a pre-group flavour to it.

Although the box at **Carluke** (above) was of almost pure Caledonian design, it was, in fact, built by the LMS before signalling matters had become standardised. It makes an interesting comparison with Lanark Junction (page 79).

Wilshamstead (below) represents the final design of LMS standard signal box. In this composite form, the brick base was styled on LNWR practice and the upper timberworks were of vaguely Midland inspiration but without the hip roof and angled off top corners to the windows. It is interesting to note that this box was built after the lever position was changed to the rear of the box in the 1930s in order to give the signalman better sighting. As this box was built in 1941 in association with a nearby ordnance supply depot, the base is slightly non-standard having 14in brickwork (without windows) for protection against possible blast.

Gable End Designs

The North Staffordshire Railway did not have a 'standard' signal box and this example at **Cresswell** was built by McKenzie and Holland. One of the end windows appears to have been replaced by one of ex-MR inspiration if not origin. An interesting ancillary feature is the pedestrian turnstile, thought to be peculiar to the NSR.

This ex-LNWR box at **Denbigh Hall** is to a design dating from the 1880s. The all-timber construction was used on embankments and this box stands near the site of the one time terminus of the London and Birmingham Railway used during the period when work was being completed at Kilsby tunnel. Note the LMS standard nameboard.

This unusual picture at **Crewe North Junction** shows the re-inforced concrete box built by the LMS just prior to the second world war to replace the old LNWR box in the background. Its construction caused the removal of the old suspension foot bridge which dated from 1878. The LNWR box, dating from 1906 when the Crewe electric type of power signalling was introduced, was built round the bridge which carried a miniature railway for the conveyance of materials from station to works. In effect, the railway passed through the box.

The LYR in its earlier days employed Saxby and Farmer as its signal contractors and the neat little box at **Parbold** (above) was to their design. The timber upperworks were to a design evolved for possible use in other locations. The box has a distinctly Scottish flavour but the nameboard is pure L & Y.

The box at **Blythe Bridge** (ex-NSR, above) was, like the example at Cresswell on the previous page, built by McKenzie and Holland and presents a remarkable contrast in style. The staircase and nameboard are, however, of much later design.

Variations on a Hip Roof Theme

Silverdale box (below) on the ex-Furness Railway line from Carnforth to Barrow was a typically neat structure. There is nothing particularly remarkable about it save, perhaps, for the rather modern looking windows; but it has a quite distinct 'cottage style' affinity with its associated station building (page 20).

At first glance, the signal box at **Way and Works Sidings** (below) is just another of typically Midland design. However, it was the only power box used on the MR, having been installed in 1905 with the Siemens electric power system. The nameboards are post-1936 LMS standard design.

Somewhat less typically Midland, by virtue of the brick base, was the massive cabin at **Spondon Station**. It was built in 1916 in conjunction with new trackwork installed for war production at the nearby factory. The box, in addition to the brick base, incorporated experiments with re-inforced concrete corner posts and mullions between the traditional MR timber sections. The central nameboard is of original MR design.

Lanark Junction presents an interesting contrast with Carluke (page 76). Although still of Caledonian inspiration, the post-group influence is present in the sense that the overall style is somewhat simplified. The box was built by the LMS in early post-group days to replace three separate boxes on the triangle between the Lanark branch and the ex-CR main line.

Keswick No. 2 Box, at the western end of Keswick station, is the original CK & P box at this location. It is clearly rather old fashioned but the steps are probably modern. Although the end nameboard is of LMS standard design, the small enamelled plate on the front of the box is probably contemporary with the main structure.

79

Two 'Lanky' Boxes

To the men of the Caledonian Railway, the 'Lanky' was the Lancaster and Carlisle Railway whose diminutive signal box at **Scout Green**, halfway up Shap Bank, is very well known to railway enthusiasts (above). This view was taken before the removal of the famous tall LNWR signal on the southbound line. The end nameboard is to LMS standard design as is the upper quadrant signal for the 'down' line.

The better known 'Lanky' was, of course, the LYR and the neat timber built signal box at **Summit Tunnel East** (left) was typical of many on this system, although a number had brick bases. The box was to a Railway Signal Company design which had been adopted as an LYR standard after responsibility for signalling work was transferred from private contractors (see page 78) to the LYR's own signal works at Horwich after 1887. Note the L & Y nameboard and signals. The 'D' shaped plate indicated (on a non-track circuited line) that when stopped at the signal, the fireman should advise the signalman by using the plunger mounted in the box at the foot of the post. Usually, these plungers were mounted on a separate pillar.

Pre-group motive power

Something over 10,000 locomotives were acquired by the LMS at the grouping in 1923. Although a policy of scrap and build was pursued by the company to the tune of almost 5,000 new standard locomotives between 1923 and 1948, there were still some 3,000 of the old timers left at the time of Nationalisation.

The pre-group locomotives represented hundreds of different classes and would make a book in themselves so this selection of but 24 examples is, perforce, somewhat, arbitrary. All that can be said is that the field for selection was deliberately confined to those locomotives which were *not* fortunate enough to be preserved.

Fox-Walker 0–6–0ST No. 1507 (above) was not among the ex-S & DJR locomotives which enjoyed a long life after absorption by the LMS in 1930. Ex-S & D No. 9, it was withdrawn in 1931. The LMS never bothered to give it a full repaint and all that happened was the obliteration of the old insignia and its replacement by new handpainted LMS characters.

Johnson ex-MR 0–4–0ST No. 1509, seen above at **Derby Works** in March 1935, was the second of its type to carry this number. At the grouping it was No. 1506 and was renumbered in 1930 (to make room for an ex-S & D locomotive), taking the number of an early withdrawal from the class. It later became the Derby Works locomotive. The bell alongside the chimney was probably fitted in order to permit its use on the Gloucester Dock Line.

The famous ex-MR Kirtley Goods was amongst the most long-lived locomotive class ever to run in Britain. The design dated from 1863 and the last survivor actually achieved a BR number. Many were the rebuilds of this famous class and this picture of No. 22567 taken at **Rugby** in August 1938 shows one of the more unusual ones. The boiler, cab and smokebox are from the Fowler era and the tender is a sort of cross-bred Kirtley/Johnson creation. The engine was withdrawn in 1946.

The Webb 2–4–2Ts with 5ft 6in drivers were introduced in 1890. By 1935, when this picture was taken at **Chester** their ranks had thinned considerably. However, 6654 (ex-LNWR 2130) was destined to become one of the very few to survive to BR days. The engine is shown in a hybrid style of livery (plain black with numbers on tanks and LMS crest on bunker), much favoured at Crewe in the early 1930s. Note, however, the LNWR lining still on the buffer beam. The engine has been fitted with replacement LMS safety valves.

0–8–2T No. 7881 (ex-LNWR 563) was one of the last survivors of 30 similar engines built between 1911 and 1917, principally for use in marshalling yards. Designed by Bowen-Cooke, they were in most essentials the tank engine equivalent of the more familiar 'G' Class 0–8–0. Only four of the 0–8–2Ts outlived the LMS and 7881 was one of them.

Ex-LNWR 2–8–0 No. 9614 (ex-LNWR 1273), seen here at **Wigan** in 1928, was built as an 0–8–0 four-cylinder compound in 1903 but converted to an 'F Class' 2–8–0 four-cylinder compound in 1906. The engine carried an 'Experiment' type boiler. Although some of the ex-LNWR 2–8–0s were converted back to 0–8–0s after the grouping, 9614 was not one of them and was withdrawn in December 1928, only five months after receiving its LMS number.

The ex-ROD 2–8–0 locomotives of Robinson Great Central design were acquired by many companies, including the LNWR, after the first world war. In consequence, the LMS found itself in possession of 50 examples of the type. Some 20 of them, in fact, were not delivered until after 1922. The example illustrated is No. 9471, seen at **Holyhead** in 1932 just prior to withdrawal. Ex-LNWR No. 2394, it became LMS 9640 in 1928 prior to being renumbered again in 1931 to make way for construction of Fowler standard Class 7F 0–8–0s.

Most North Staffordshire Railway locomotives were neat and unfussy machines built in the company workshops. Occasionally, however, the railway bought locomotives from outside contractors. One such example was No. 1603 (ex-NSR 75), one of a pair of rather ungainly 0–6–0Ts acquired from Kerr Stuart in 1919. The LMS was not very enthusiastic about them, even though they were but four years old, and both had gone by 1933.

Of much more characteristic NSR design was Class 'E' 0–6–0 No. 8656 (ex-NSR 111, 1st LMS 2329). The design, by Clare, dated from 1871 and the engines had a long life. The LMS originally numbered them in the 23xx series but the introduction of the Fowler 2–6–4Ts caused them to be renumbered in the 86xx series adjacent to the ex-LNWR 0–6–0s. No. 8656 was withdrawn in 1930 and the picture was taken at **Crewe** shortly before this date.

The LYR was one of the largest operators of 2–4–2Ts in the country and owned almost 3CO examples of the type at the grouping. This picture of 10899 (ex-LYR 1545), although taken at **Arksey** on the ex-GNR main line just north of Doncaster in May 1936, is typical of many trains to be seen on and around the Central Division of the LMS at that time. The train was working to Doncaster via Knottingley from Wakefield, where the locomotive was based. Although an ex-LYR 2–4–2T is preserved, it is a different variety from 10899 which was the long bunkered version with non-superheated belpaire boiler and extended smokebox.

The Barton Wright ex-LYR 0–6–2Ts of 1881 design did not long survive the grouping, all being scrapped by 1932. In this view, No. 11612 (ex-LYR 688) is seen shortly after the grouping. At the time this picture was taken the engine was still carrying LYR lining and the new LMS number had been crudely hand painted over the space vacated by the LYR numberplate.

Although they were nick-named 'Teddy Bears', one feels that some sort of elephantine soubriquet would have been equally appropriate for the ex-LYR large boilered 0–8–0s, for they were surely the most enormous looking of all the pre-group locomotives. The example illustrated, No. 12971 (ex-LYR 738) of Lower Darwen shed was, in fact, a Hughes rebuild of an earlier small boilered Aspinall 0–8–0. Although many of these locomotives were withdrawn relatively early in LMS days, 12791 lasted until 1949, only two years before the class became extinct.

84

Passenger services on the old North London Railway, later absorbed into the LNWR, were operated in pre-group days by a most distinctive series of 4–4–0Ts, some of whose earliest members dated back to the 1860s. They were all, therefore, somewhat ancient by the time of the grouping and the LMS proceeded to break them up with great vigour. A few, however, managed at least to receive LMS numbers, if not LMS livery, before being put to the torch. One such example was No. 6466 (ex-NLR 37, LNWR 2830) seen here circa 1924/5 with its full pre-group lining and only the LMS number to indicate new ownership. It was scrapped in March 1926.

The Maryport and Carlisle Railway was one of the smallest companies to come into the LMS group. Most of its engines did not last very long after 1922, but all four members of its class of 0–4–2 tender engines (designed by Smellie in 1879) soldiered on until 1928. One example of the class, No. 10013 (ex-M&CR 16) is seen here outside **Upperby** shed. Note that originally two extra buffers were fitted at a lower level on the front buffer beam to enable the engine to work at colleries using the old chauldron wagons. In spite of this provision, the engine was classified as a passenger type and finished in the LMS lined crimson lake livery.

Other than the ubiquitous 0–6–0 tender type, the most common locomotive wheel arrangement favoured by the Furness Railway was the 0–6–2T of which it had 23, all designed by Pettigrew. Three variations existed, of which the most common type is represented by 11638 (ex-FR 109), seen here at **Moor Row** in July 1932. The locomotive was still in pre-1928 livery at the time the picture was taken and was withdrawn in early 1933, so it is unlikely it ever received the later LMS style of painting.

Caledonian 4–4–0 types were legion and the famous Dunalastair series was well known to railway enthusiasts. However, before McIntosh introduced these locomotives, Dugald Drummond had already provided the CR with quite a number of extremely neat 4–4–0 designs of which CR No. 1081 is seen here. This was Drummond's first design of 4–4–0 for the 'Caley' and set the style, as it were, for the whole generations of 4–4–0s which were to follow. This picture is interesting in showing the locomotive in pre-group livery several years after grouping. Withdrawn in 1930, it is thought not to have received its allotted LMS number 14109.

4–6–0 No. 17914 (ex-CR 188) was a member of the Caledonian Railway '179' Class, designed by McIntosh in 1913. These engines were the freight equivalent, more or less, of the famous 'Cardean' Class 4–6–0 passenger locomotives. Like most ex-CR 4–6–0s, the '179 Class' was not a long lived design after the grouping and 17914 was only 21 years old when withdrawn in 1935. Like so many other pre-group classes, they were simply no match for the Stanier Class 5.

Before Drummond and McIntosh had put their indelible stamp upon Caledonian locomotive design, the characteristic lineaments of Connor and Brittain were more common. Amongst the few survivals to the LMS of this earlier era were the attractive 0–4–2s designed by Brittain in 1878. No. 17013 (ex-CR 279) is seen here in pre-1928 LMS freight livery. This was one of the longer lasting members of the class, not being withdrawn until 1931.

Quite a different concept of 0–4–2 locomotive was represented by No. 17060 (ex-GSWR No. 254), seen in pre-1928 LMS livery at **Hurlford** in September 1926. This was a member of quite a numerous class of 1901–3 vintage Manson rebuilds of an earlier 1874 Stirling design. Note the absence of a coupling on the front buffer beam. Apart from the engine, this picture also depicts a venerable outside framed ex-GSWR goods brake and a wonderfully ornate water column.

Hugh Smellie came to the GSWR from the Maryport and Carlisle Railway and his 0–6–0 design represented here bore a certain resemblance to his M&CR 0–4–2s (page 85), although the domeless boiler is more reminiscent of Stirling's GSWR engines of the 1870s. No. 17129 was ex-GSWR 560 and was withdrawn in 1930.

The 2–6–0 tender engine was a rarity on LMS lines until the advent of LMS standard designs and only the CR and GSWR possessed examples of the type. The GSWR had the larger number and No. 17829 (ex-GSWR 60) is seen here at **Kingmoor** shed (its home base) during the 1930s. The class was designed in 1915 by Peter Drummond, who came to the GSWR from the Highland in 1912, and enjoyed quite a long post-grouping life by GSWR standards. No. 17829 was, in fact, the last survivor, being withdrawn in 1947.

Drummond engines, whichever member of that distinguished family had designed them, all had a strong family resemblance and Peter Drummond's designs for the Highland Railway between 1896 and 1911 were no exception. An early design was the 'Small Ben' class of 4–4–0 locomotives of which the pioneer example No. 14397 (ex-HR No. 1) **Ben-y-Gloe** is depicted here. In the background is an ex-LNWR brake van.

In 1900, Peter Drummond introduced the Highland's one and only 0–6–0 tender engine design. Its physical resemblance to its Caledonian cousins designed by Dugald Drummond was quite remarkable and like the Caledonian types, it was a long lived design. No. 17704 (ex-HR 37) was the last of the class to be built and was withdrawn in late 1946. Known for some reason as 'Barneys', the Highland 0–6–0s became extinct in 1952.

Peter Drummond's final design for the HR was an 0–6–4T evolved primarily for banking duties between Blair Atholl and Druimuachdar summit. No. 15301 (ex-HR 66) is seen here on the turntable at **Blair Atholl** in the early 1930s. It was withdrawn in 1934.

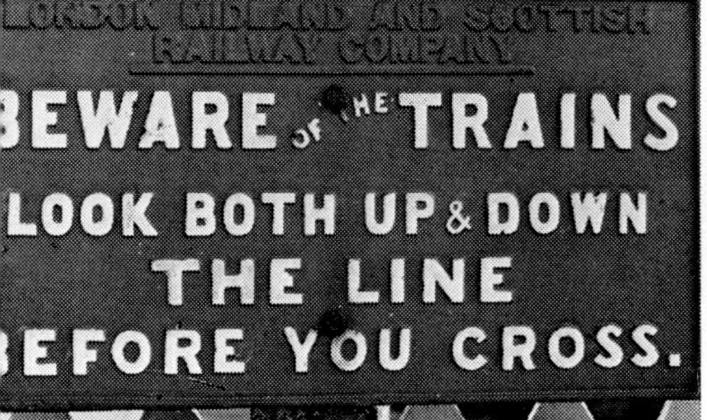

Lineside furniture

The LMS existed for only 25 years and much of the ancillary equipment it inherited from the pre-group companies was perfectly capable of lasting for that length of time. However, when notices and the like had to be replaced, the LMS employed its own designs.

Above are shown examples of both cast and enamelled LMS standard notices. In LMS days, the cast notices were "officially" painted with black letters against a white ground, but cream/yellow backgrounds were quite common. The enamel signs were white on black.

The most commonly occurring LMS standard sign was the 'Hawkseye' station nameboard. In this case, something of a deliberate attempt to replace pre-group signs seems to have been made and the new nameboards were to be seen all over the system. They were mounted in wooden frames and almost always cast in a fairly light alloy. **Keighley** (below, right), photographed in BR condition, also exhibits the auxiliary sign denoting the presence of refreshment facilities at the station. The LMS colour scheme was black letters against a yellow ground. This yellow background was often made of a mixture of glass and pigment to give it a semi-translucent appearance at night.

There were odd exceptions to the normal type and **Elm Park** was one of them (left, below). In this case, the wood frame was of normal pattern but the nameboard itself appears to be either enamelled or painted.

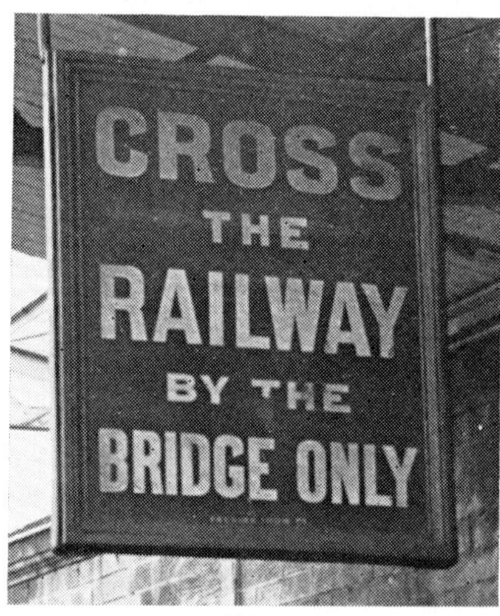

(a) Platform seat at **Gatley** for Cheadle—ex-LNWR.
(b) Furness Railway platform seat at **Bootle**.
(c) Conventional intermediate ex-MR milepost 70¼ at **Hardingstone Junction**.
(d) Ex-MR intermediate milepost for branch lines. This one is at **Haworth** and the post indicates 3¾ miles from Keighley.
(e) Ex-MR principal milepost 53 on the Bedford–Northampton line.
(f) Ex-Maryport and Carlisle water column at **Aspatria**.
(g) Ex-SMJR notice at **Kineton**.
(h) Ex-Caledonian notice at **Hamilton**.

90

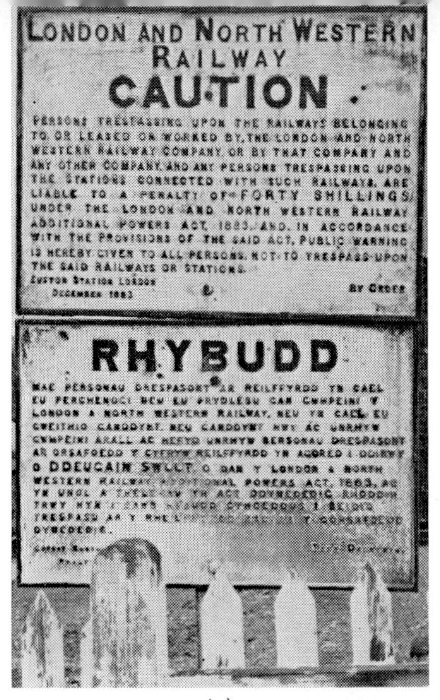

(a)   (b)   (c)

(d)   (e)   (f)

(g)   (h)   (j)

(a) Ex-LNWR bi-lingual trespass notice at **Rhydymwyn**.

(b) Ex-Furness Railway lattice post with LMS upper quadrant arm—**Silverdale**.

(c) Pre-group lower quadrant signal with LMS upper quadrant distant arm mounted below it, acting as a fixed distant—**Woodend** (ex-FR).

(d) Ex-LNWR bridge notices.

(e) LMS sleeper mounted track circuit plate.

(f) Ex-NSR trespass sign near **Blythe Bridge**.

(g) Ex-Furness trespass notice—**Arnside**.

(h) Ex-MR engine stop board—**Derby**.

(j) Ex-MR bridge notice—**Silsden**.

In 1929, Parliament approved the LMS road traffic act which was the pilot legislation for similar acts for the other railways. This enabled railways to increase activities beyond feeder services to include the carriage of both passengers and goods between places which were not rail connected. The most obvious manifestation of this act was the operation of bus services. The first vehicles in the new LMS bus fleet were 20 Leyland Lions which were purchased in almost 'off the peg' condition—an unusual practice in those days for the railway. A roof rack and ladder were, however, fitted for luggage at a later date.

On the other road

Although the growth of long distance road haulage has had serious effects upon the railway system of the British Isles, the railways have traditionally relied upon *short* distance road transport of some sort or another in order to convey merchandise of all kinds to and from the nearest railhead. During the 19th Century, the customary agency for this service was the horse drawn dray in one of its many varieties. However, the first world war gave tremendous impetus to the development of the internal combustion engine and by the time the LMS came on the scene, the motor age had moved out of the childhood stage. Even though the LMS continued to make extensive use of horse drawn vehicles (see pages 99/104), it was not slow to realise the value of motorised road transport and its fleet of road vehicles was considerably larger and more varied than at first may be generally realised.

As might be expected, some of these vehicles were basically used to replace the old horse and cart, but the company also experimented with other uses for road vehicles. Some of the many ramifications of the LMS road motor scene are depicted on this and the next few pages.

92

The LMS went to considerable trouble to illustrate its domestic removal container services in the 1930s. The containers themselves had elaborate eye-catching liveries and several photographs were taken of actual contracts being carried out in the home counties area. The venerable AEC (above), has seen two or three major rebuilds and has obviously been spruced up for the event. White wall tyres were not normally the order of the day! Originally, this type of lorry was fitted with solid wheels and a canvas topped open front cab. Additional load capacity has been provided by a converted horse trailer and was achieved by fitting a draw bar in lieu of shafts and rubber instead of steel shod wheels. It may also have had some form of braking. The presence of the motor car in the picture was, it is believed, an attempt to make the point that the furniture owners themselves did not have to travel by rail!

The picture below shows a container being loaded with furniture. It is secured to the platform of a Karrier which was an example of the first type of cab-over-engine lorry used by the LMS. Originally solid tyred and without windscreen, these lorries were so early that access to the cab was not by the conventional side door. The first cab door was on the front at the nearside with a stirrup alongside the radiator. This door then became radiussed on plan view and finally, both front corners of the cab were rounded off and became doors.

Express parcels traffic often merited the most up to date road vehicles and the smart turnout of the Dennis van (above) is a credit to both coach builder and coach painter. Note the seriffed and shaded lettering and lined panels combined with wartime markings. This type of short wheelbase vehicle was developed jointly by the vehicle manufacturers and the railways so that it could operate in confined railway yards. Similar vehicles were produced by Karrier and Scammell. The driver is priming the engine with domestic gas as part of a wartime petrol economy scheme. The vehicle to the left is a heavier Albion van.

By complete contrast, the lower view shows a Wolverton bodied Albion four ton van. In the opinion of many people, these were the most handsome commercial vehicles owned by the LMS. The picture shows it being used to ship National Art Treasures to safety during the war.

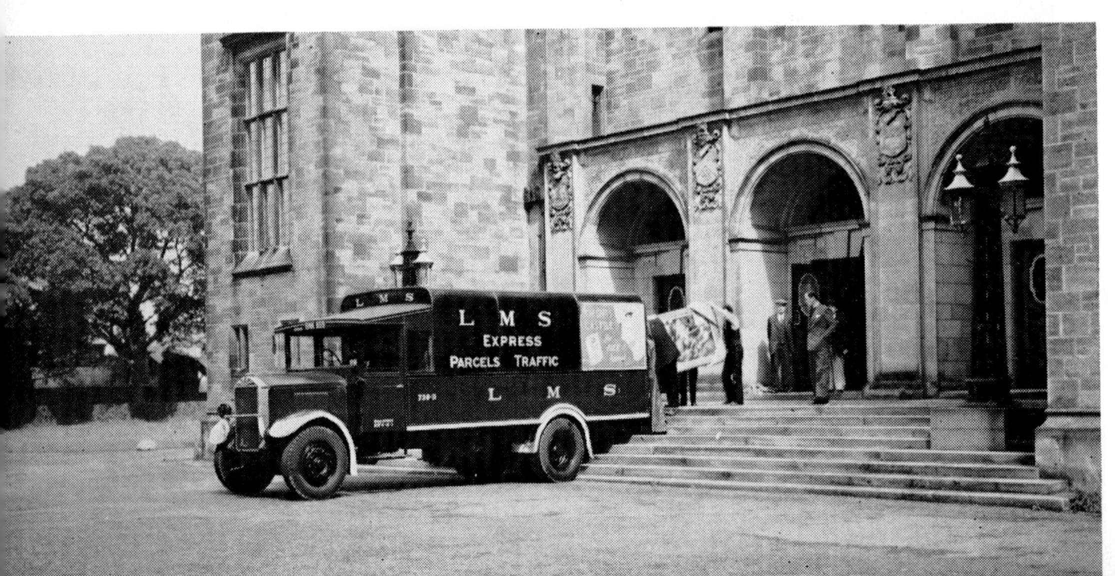

No pictorial survey of railway road vehicles would be complete without a picture of a mechanical horse. Originally developed to replace the four legged horse in light delivery work, it was rapidly developed to take the heaviest loads. The Scammell horse and trailer (above) is about to receive a large loaded container scaling somewhere about six tons. The crane in the background is typical of the self-propelled transhipment cranes built for the LMS. The jib and winch arrangement remained almost constant until well into BR days. The earlier models were mounted on a turntable on a three axle lorry chassis but later models were mounted direct onto four wheels and traversed by moving the whole vehicle.

The lower illustration illustrates the main object of using mechanical horses and trailers, One trailer and container is being unloaded while the horse is removing an empty container. Ideally the object would be to have a third (loaded) trailer for this horse at the railhead. The prime mover in this case is an intermediate design by Karrier. The location is Boots warehouse, **Blackburn**.

Heavy lorries died hard on the LMS and the unidentified example (above) was probably inherited from one of the pre-group companies who, in turn, had purchased it as WD surplus after the first world war. It probably received its Derby style cab, with near side only door, early in LMS days and had not been altered since. It is almost beyond belief that in the early thirties this solid tyred monster could still be running about with only oil lamps and but two wheels braked !

The 'H' type container was developed with an eye to the conveyance of building materials (left and below, left). In the first illustration, a lorry load of tiles, packed into the containers at the manufacturers, is being exchanged for empty containers from a rail wagon. In the second illustration, containers are being unloaded from the lorry and hoisted directly to where they are needed on the building site which is, of course, **Euston House**— probably the largest single example of LMS architecture. The lorries are both AECs of basically similar type and had, at the date of the pictures, been rebuilt or modified several times. One has oil sidelights and other electric.

The LMS railway ran examples of practically every Morris Commercial vehicle produced. Morris established themselves as the foremost British manufacturer of light commercials in the pre-war era—in fact, very few other vehicle manufactuerers bothered with the light commercial in the 1920s. In consequence vehicles of this class were either Morris Commercial, foreign products or foreign sponsored products such as Ford. In order to combat unemployment, 'Buy British' became the cry of the day and most national users of light vehicles, such as the railways and the GPO, used Morris Commercials. In the pictures above, a fairly early example of the three axle Morris is seen on two different occasions in the **Macclesfield** area. This vehicle was originally fitted with an open fronted cab but has had a windscreen added.

Not all LMS road vehicles plied from rail head to other points. The railway did, in fact, undertake any form of cartage, some of which never got anywhere near the rails. Two broadly 'agricultural' examples are depicted in the pictures above. On the left, three standard Bedford lorries are seen being used to collect milk from farms for delivery to a cheese factory.

The LMS had a sizeable fleet of heavy duty tip lorries. These were variously used for coal, mineral and other traffic and one of the rarer tipper duties was the shipping of the sugar beet crop—usually but not always to the rail head. The lorry is a Karrier and to encourage the use of railway owned vehicles, the LMS also supplied the mechanical loading shovel.

Handling the freight

Freight was the most important kind of traffic on most routes of the LMS system and the company classified its freight traffic into various different categories, each category being precisely defined in the General Appendix to the LMS Working Timetables. This study of LMS freight traffic is, in part, based on these official definitions and the class of train was indicated, visually, by the headlamps carried by the locomotive.

The striking picture above, taken from the footplate of the leading engine of a double headed freight ascending from Carr Bridge to **Slocht Summit** (ex-HR) just after nationalisation shows Class 5 No. 45478 running in direct contravention of the regulation which said 'When a train running on the LMS Railway is worked by two engines attached in front of the train, the second engine must not carry headlamps'! The picture on the left shows a brake van at the rear of an empty wagon train at **Hatch End.** Its tail lamps are arranged in accordance with the rules for three or four main lines viz: 'On the slow, goods or loop lines . . .. One red side light on the side of the van furthest away from the fast line, one white side light on the side of the van nearest the fast line and one red tail light.'

In the next few pages, we have tried to show something of the organisation and end product of this 'other half' of the LMS.

98

Above is shown a panoramic view of the famous **Toton** up yard in early LMS days. The vast quantities of coal wagons are ready for shipment to Brent. Most of them are local area Private Owner wagons with a scattering of company vehicles but there are one or two strangers—e.g. Bradford and Sons of Yeovil in the centre of the picture. The high level lines from Trent can just be discerned in the left background of the picture.

Below is shown the 'forwarded' side of the goods depot at **Birmingham Lawley Street** in September 1945. 'Forwarded Traffic' was the railway term for goods going out and the view is taken looking down No. 2 Cart Road. Note that in spite of the use of the mobile battery crane for loading the wagons in a more up to date fashion, horse drawn vehicles are still much in evidence. This was probably a legacy from the war years when the replacement of horses was slowed down in order to save valuable imports of petrol for the motor fleet.

Mail and Parcels

It is a moot point whether mail and parcels traffic should be included in the freight section. However, the three trains on this page were most certainly not carrying passengers !

At the head of the page, the down West Coast Postal is seen carrying express passenger head-code as it approaches the pick up point at **Harrow** on 29th May 1947. The locomotive is Stanier Jubilee Class 4–6–0 No. 5659 **Drake** in fully lined 1946 livery.

To carry the head lamps in the position depicted in the other two pictures on this page, the train had to be a 'Parcels, news-paper, fish, meat, fruit, milk, horse or perishable train, com-posed of coaching stock'. The upper view shows ex-LNWR Prince of Wales Class 4–6–0 No. 25678 **Milton** (ex-LNWR 2055) with a milk train at **Ashton** on 30th June 1934. The train carried both bulk liquid milk (in the tanks) and milk in churns in the vans. This picture was taken before the use of exclusively six-wheel milk tanks became mandatory (1937).

At the foot of the page is a more conventional parcels train consisting of an interesting variety of vehicles. The leading vehicle is one of the ex-LNWR 50ft full brakes built in 1908, originally for use in the American Special boat trains. It is followed by an ex-MR bogie brake, two ex-MR outside framed six-wheelers and an ex-LNWR arc roofed 50ft brake. The locomotive is ex-MR Johnson 'Belpaire' Class 3P 4–4–0 No. 707.

100

Fitted Freight

A 'fitted freight' was classified in the LMS book as a freight, fish or cattle train with the continuous brake in use on *not less* than one-third the vehicles. To qualify as a fitted train, the continuous brake pipe had to run from locomotive to Brake Van, even if some of the vehicles were themselves devoid of vacuum brakes.

The train shown at the head of the page, although an early BR example, shows a typical fitted freight climbing **Shap** behind Class 5 No. 45296 and banked by Fowler Class 4P 2–6–4T No. 42404. The train differs little from those which could be seen at the close of the LMS period. By complete contrast, the second picture, taken at **Glasgow St Enoch** in early LMS days shows red liveried ex-GSWR 4–4–0 No. 14135 (ex-GSWR 795) about to leave with what looks rather like a conventional parcels train of ex-MR stock. However, the fitted freight headlamp code indicates that some, at least, of the vehicles in the train were not classified as coaching stock.

The last picture shows a fitted cattle train on the ex-MR main line during the early 1930s. The locomotive is ex-LNWR Claughton Class 4–6–0 No. 5955 (ex-LNWR 1103) and is in original small boilered condition. It has, however, been fitted with a replacement ROD tender.

Express Freight

The LMS had two classifications for express freight trains. If there were less than one third but four or more fitted vehicles at the head of the train, it was generally referred to as a 'Maltese freight—an allusion to the Maltese Cross symbol used in the working timetable to distinguish them from their less exalted brethren with less than four fitted vehicles. This lower category of express freight did not necessarily include fitted vehicles at all, but was not allowed to include vehicles other than those fitted with oil axleboxes.

The first example of an express freight (above) shows an unidentified ex-LNWR 0–8–0 passing **Nuneaton** No. 1 box during the war with a train of sheeted down army tanks carried on 'Warwells'— special well wagons built for WD use during the second world war.

In the second picture, a 'Maltese' freight of early post group vintage is seen leaving **Carlisle** headed by ex-Caledonian 'River' Class 4–6–0 No. 14761 (ex-CR 943). The fitted 'head' appears to consist of six or seven vehicles. The River class of engines were built to a Highland Railway order but only two had been delivered and neither had entered regular service when the HR civil engineer forbade their use on the grounds that they were too heavy. The Caledonian purchased them and got a very good engine for the money.

The last picture, taken near **Lancaster** in the early 1930s, is probably another 'Maltese' freight but it is not possible to be certain whether or not sufficient of the leading vehicles are fitted. The engines are ex-MR Class 3F 0–6–0 No. 3231 and ex-LYR Aspinall 0–6–0 No. 12225 (ex-LYR 315)—a somewhat unusual combination of motive power.

Through Freight

The 'one-over-one' headcode defined a 'Through freight train, or ballast train conveying workmen and running not less than 15 miles without stopping'. It covered a whole variety of workings, three of which are shown here.

Above, Stanier Class 8F No. 8154 is seen leaving the down loops at **Hellifield** (ex-MR) with a northbound through freight from Blackburn which had worked up over the ex-LYR line through Clitheroe and Gisburn. This is a fairly late LMS picture, unlike the second view which shows an early ex-Caledonian example, mostly consisting of open wagons. In fact, it looks so much like a mineral train that one wonders why it was not so classified. The engines are first and last generation Caledonian 0–6–0s. The train engine (No. 17360, ex-CR 556) is a Drummond 'Jumbo' of the mid-1880s and the leading locomotive (No. 17690, ex-CR 677) is the final Pickersgill development of the 1918–20 period.

The lower picture was taken near **Beighton** on the original North Midland main line between Chesterfield and Rotherham (avoiding Sheffield) and shows ex-MR Class 3F 0–6–0 No. 3364 at the head of a mixed assortment of wagons. Note that in a train consisting of a variety of vehicles, cattle wagons, if loaded, had to be marshalled against the engine.

SCOTTISH RAILWAY C? COTTON
L M S
BARNSLEY
MAIN
520
OLDHAM
INDUSTRIAL
SOCIETY
WELSH GRANITE C? L?
PENMAENMAWR

L M S
1353
L M S

The Town Goods Yard

It is hard to believe that such scenes as are depicted on this page were once a commonplace in almost every town of any size in the kingdom. Here were the yards from whence the railway derived so much of its traffic until the motor vehicle had made many of them redundant.

The double page spread shows the ex-LYR yard at **Oldham Werneth** in pre-war days. The massive multi-storey goods warehouses were found all over the Lancashire and Yorkshire system and were by no means confined to the larger towns. This particular specimen is, however, a particularly large one. Note that most of the uncovered area of the yard is devoted to coal traffic, the general merchandise vehicles being mostly confined to the under cover shed adjacent to the warehouse.

Note also the completely separate covered warehouse for cotton.

Across the Pennines, wool took the place of cotton as is obvious from the quantities of baled wool seen in the lower picture (opposite) which shows **Bradford Bridge Street** *circa* 1932. In this picture the absence of coal wagons is as noticeable as is their presence in the picture of Oldham. Two particularly interesting points can be made about the picture. Firstly is the presence of no fewer than 30 horse drawn road vehicles by contrast with but one or two of the motorised variety. The second point of interest is that the great variety of goods vehicles includes a considerable proportion of open wagons, including one still in LNWR livery.

Miscellaneous Freight

Although the term 'mineral train' covered almost any type of material derived from the earth's crust, by far the most important single commodity was coal. Of all the lines incorporated into the LMS, there can have been few more important coal routes than the ex-LYR main line which linked the rich Yorkshire coalfield with the factories and mills of Lancashire.

Above, LMS standard Class 4F No. 4128 is seen passing **Luddendenfoot** troughs as it returns to Yorkshire with a long train of coal empties on 7th September 1945. For some reason it is carrying express freight headcode rather than the single lamp over the right buffer which was the code for empty wagons. The same single lamp code also denoted loaded minerals and is seen (left) displayed on ex-LNWR Class G2A 0–8–0 No. 9094 (ex-LNWR 1556) as it, too, passes Luddendenfoot, heading towards Lancashire with a loaded coal train on the same day in 1945.

At the top of this page, the empty wagon/loaded mineral headcode is also displayed on ex-LYR Aspinall 0–6–0 No. 12397 (ex-LYR 492) at the head of what looks nothing like a train satisfying either definition! While it is conceivable that the leading container is empty and, indeed, the van, the sheeted down open wagons further down the train suggest that the vehicles were loaded. The engine was shedded at Rugby at the time of this picture (October 1938) and the train is seen at **Northampton.**

The local stopping freight is almost a thing of the past but time was when the length of these trains reached quite large proportions as is exemplified in the picture of ex-CR '908' Class 4–6–0 No. 14616 (ex-CR 915) at the head of a stopping freight in early LMS days. The locomotive is in pre-1928 LMS passenger livery.

The efforts made by the LMS in promoting the growth of container traffic have already been mentioned on page 93. The picture below was specially taken to help promote and publicise the services and shows five furniture containers secured to a variety of one plank open wagons (one still in LNWR livery). The train is headed by Hughes/Fowler 'Crab' type 2–6–0 No. 13119, later 2819.

Final Round-up

From time to time, special freights would be commissioned. Such an example is shown in the upper view taken at **Uttoxeter** in 1929. It shows ex-North Staffordshire Class 'L' 0–6–2T No. 2258 (ex-NSR 89) at the head of a special train conveying 40 loads of Bamford's Agricultural Implements from Uttoxeter to Harrogate for the Royal Agricultural Show 1929.

No survey of freight and associated workings would be complete without a look at those other duties which, although not gaining revenue for the company, were essential for keeping the traffic moving. The first example (left) shows ex-LNWR 'Cauliflower' No. 8529 (ex-LNWR 166) shunting empty carriages at **Birmingham New Street** in May 1938. By complete contrast, the ex-MR breakdown train is shown in the lower picture, shortly after grouping. In fact, only the engine, ex-MR Class 3 0–6–0 No. 3637, bears evidence of LMS ownership. The train is seen standing in front of the ex-North Staffordshire Goods Station at **Derby**.

Finally, we come to the all important business of track maintenance. Above is seen ex-LNWR 'George the Fifth' Class 4–4–0 No. 5367 **Traveller** (ex-LNWR 2089) at **Lea Road** troughs with a ballast train on 4th May 1936. It will be noted that the lamp displayed on the buffer beam is wrong. If the engine is propelling the train it should have a centrally mounted red lamp and if it is operating engine first the single headlamp indicating 'ballast train requiring to stop in section' should be over the left hand buffer.

The Derby weed killing train (right) consisted of two ex-LNWR tenders, a four wheel 'Tarmac' tank wagon and a modified ex-MR brake van. Note the extra pipework below the brake van headstock.

The lower picture shows a very different kind of ballast train to that in the upper view. It shows the use of hopper wagons and the method of ballast spreading using a ballast brake fitted with plough. Note the presence of a conventional brake at the end of the train.

Au revoir LMS?

The last day of existence of the LMS was, technically, the 31st December 1947 and the heading picture shows the last LMS train leaving **St. Pancras** at 11.50 p.m. on that day headed by Jubilee Class 4–6–0 No. 5614 **Leeward Islands** appropriately still wearing the red livery. Shortly afterwards, there began the obliteration of the old marks of ownership. Is it imagination or was there really a smile on the face of the painter as a Compound received the treatment at Derby in May 1948?

But was the LMS *really* finished? In spite of everything, it fell to ex-LMS engines to bear the brunt of the 'Farewell to Steam' operations during that fateful month, August 1968, when steam hauled trains ran, officially, for the last time on British Railways standard gauge lines. Opposite two faithful Stanier Black 5s travel light to Carlisle over **Arten Gill** viaduct on the Settle and Carlisle main line prior to working the last special train on 11th August.

Nationalisation was probably as essential for the British railways as was the final suppression of steam; but while Shap Fell is still there along with 6201 and several of her smaller sisters, there must be grounds for hope. Maybe the ghost of Sir William Stanier will, one day, have the last laugh after all. For our part we prefer not to say 'Farewell' but merely AU REVOIR!

Sources of illustrations

V. R. Anderson	20 (except top), 76, 77 (top), 78 (except bottom right), 79 (top, middle), 89 (middle left and right, bottom right), 90 (all except top right and bottom centre), 91 (all except top right, bottom right and centre)
Authors' Collections	14 (top, middle), 28 (except top left), 33 (bottom left), 34 (top right), 36 (middle, bottom), 37 (bottom), 38 (bottom), 39, 42 (bottom), 45 (bottom), 46 (middle), 51 (middle, bottom), 65 (middle), 81 (top), 82 (bottom), 83 (bottom), 84 (bottom), 85 (top, middle), 86 (top, bottom), 101 (bottom), 109 (middle)
British Rail	Frontispiece, 6, 11, 12 (top), 13 (top), 15, 17 (top), 18 (bottom), 19, 21, 22 (bottom), 23–27, 29–31, 32 (bottom), 33 (top left and right), 34 (bottom left), 35, 40, 42 (top), 43, 44 (bottom), 48 (bottom), 49, 52 (top), 53, 56–57, 59, 60 (top, middle), 63, 64, 65 (top, bottom), 66, 72, 74 (top), 75 (top, middle), 77 (middle, bottom), 78 (bottom right), 80, 89 (bottom left), 92–97, 98 (bottom), 99, 101 (top), 102 (top), 103 (top), 104, 105, 107 (bottom), 108 (top, bottom), 109 (bottom), 110
H. C. Casserley	18 (top), 28 (top left), 41, 52 (bottom), 69, 73, 85 (bottom)
T. J. Edgington	60 (bottom), 61 89 (top left)
A. G. Ellis	33 (bottom right), 37 (middle), 38 (top, middle), 46 (bottom), 51 (top), 54, 68, 82 (middle), 84 (top, middle), 87 (top, middle), 101 (middle), 102 (middle), 103 (middle, bottom), 107 (middle)
R. J. Essery	90 (bottom middle)
W. L. Good	50 (bottom)
L. Hanson	81 (middle, bottom), 100 (middle), 107 (top), 108 (middle)
D. Jenkinson	20 (top), 79 (bottom), 89 (top right), 90 (top right), 91 (top right, bottom right)
L & GRP	50 (top), 74 (bottom), 75 (bottom)
Photomatic Ltd.	9, 45 (middle), 83 (top, middle), 86 (middle), 87 (bottom), 88, 100 (bottom)
G. H. Platt	82 (top)
W. G. Rear	111
F. W. Shuttleworth	58
Derek Smith	91 (bottom centre)
H. Gordon Tidey	36 (top), 37 (top), 102 (bottom)
Bishop Eric Treacy	44 (top), 45 (top), 47 (bottom), 48 (top), 50 (middle), 52 (middle)
A. E West	32 (top left, top right)
E. R. Wethersett	10, 12 (bottom), 13 (bottom), 16, 55, 62, 100 (top), 106, 109 (top)
The late C. White	67
Gavin L. Wilson	8, 14 (bottom), 17 (bottom), 22 (top), 34 (middle right), 46 (top), 47 (top), 98 (top)

To all the above individuals and organisations we offer our sincere and grateful thanks.